ETHICS AND ETHOLOGY
FOR A HAPPY DOG

Anders Hallgren

ETHICS AND ETHOLOGY FOR A HAPPY DOG

CADMOS

Cover photo: Dr. Richard Maurer

The publisher and the author are not liable for any
damage to persons and property that may be incurred
in connection with the implementation and application
of the exercises and methods described in this book.
Although these were designed and tested with great
care, they should always be carried out with due
circumspection.

IMPRINT

Copyright © 2015 Cadmos Publishing Limited,
Richmond, UK
Copyright of original edition © 2014 Cadmos Verlag
GmbH, Schwarzenbek, Germany

Design: www.ravenstein2.de
Setting: Das Agenturhaus, Munich
Content photos: Dr. Richard Maurer, Shutterstock.com

Translation: Susanne Wigforss
Editorial: Maren Müller
Printed by Graspo CZ, a.s., Czech Republic,
www.graspo.com

British Library Cataloguing in Publication Data.
A catalogue record of this book is available from the
British Library.

Printed in the Czech Republic

ISBN: 978-0-85788-017-8

CONTENT

CONTENT

Preface

This book is intended to be a guide on how to have the best possible relationship with your dog, how to interact, activate, lead and just socialize and have fun together. The advice given is based on a purely ethical approach, in many cases based on animal protection laws, rules and recommendations by the authorities, but also guided by common sense and general compassion. Furthermore, the recommendations are based on modern ethology, which has taught us about dogs' natural lives and needs. This advice also takes into consideration what the psychology of learning has shown is the best way to train a dog – whether it is about teaching the dog something new or to stop it from doing something.

We live in a world flooded with information and advice about dogs, how we should live with them and fix various behavioural problems. Some people still argue that harsh training methods are just natural and claim that they are not brutal. To defend their case they use confusing terms such as:

"You have to be a better leader."

"You must be obvious and straightforward."

"You have to assume responsibility and take charge."

"You cannot hand over the responsibility to the dog."

Others believe that you should not be harsh and that you should refrain from punishing a dog. Instead, you should have a positive demeanour and use positive training methods.

It is easy for a dog owner to get confused. What is right and what is wrong? People may try different methods and listen to all kinds of advice. Although it feels uncomfortable, they might even try harsher training methods, which usually give short-term results, but the problems soon return.

In this book, you will find simple and practical recommendations on how to train your dog ethically using "soft" methods. Today, you will find that there is plenty of scientific proof that the proponents for "soft" methods are right. It is my firm belief that you should train your dog using rewards and positive methods and avoid punishment and conflict with your dog. What you would not dream of doing to your child, you should not do to your dog.

Anders Hallgren
Järna, Sweden 2014

9

(Photo: Shutterstock)

Your dog —
A TRUE FRIEND

We all know that a dog is man's best friend. Furthermore, dogs are very much like us. Surprising, but true: We have around 75 percent of our genes in common! Just like us, a dog is a social animal to whom family is most important. Dogs also mark and protect their territory, although not like us with garden fences and warning signs. For that purpose dogs use other strategies, such as barking and urine marking. A dog keeps contact and communicates a lot with us, unfortunately much more than we are able to perceive and understand. The dog defends us if it suspects we are in danger, it tries to make us get along as a family, and it is even capable of warning us about a fire long before a mechanical fire alarm would go off. Having a dog around also makes you feel good, it gives children a feeling of safety and has been proven to have real health benefits, especially for older people.

Dogs pay particular attention to their close and social relationships and they go to great lengths to ensure their stability. They protect each other, groom and play, and seek body contact while resting. These are common behaviours among dogs that know each other well, and also between dogs and their human family members.

(Photo: Shutterstock)

13

In order for us to understand where this comes from, we need to look at the dog's ancestors – the wolves. Life in the wild is incredibly tough. It is believed that a wolf in the wild only lives until the age of five or six years because of the harsh demands of a life out there (9). Knowing this, it is easy to understand why wolf packs with good relationships, in which they protect and take care of each other, also have a better chance of survival.

Observations have shown that the psychological bonds among individuals in a wolf family are so important that the family members display a number of specific behaviours to enforce these bonds. In addition, behaviours that can weaken these essential bonds, for example various forms of aggression, are very rare.

Collective bonding behaviours

Like wolves, our dogs have many different behaviours for contact and bonding within their pack and we probably only know about a few of them by now. In the future, I am sure that we will discover many more of these important behaviours, such as quick glances and small, low sounds, various forms of friendly body contact and different ways of grooming.

Nose contact

We all notice this behaviour in our dogs. If our relationship is good, nose contact is short and frequent, mostly directed to hands and arms, but also to other parts of the body.

The late ethologist and wolf researcher Erik Zimen noticed that roaming wolves often use nose-to-fur contact as frequently as every tenth minute. He concluded that all wolves used such frequent contact to strengthen their bonds within the pack (35).

The behaviour often consists of extremely short glances and a very light touch of the nose against the other's fur, so lightly that the other wolf does not even seem to register it.

Immediately after the nose-to-fur contact, it seems as though it never even happened. If the wolf who was touched looks at the one who did it, the latter just looks straight ahead or to the side, as if he wanted to say: "Don't look at me. I didn't do it". Just like when another person teasingly pokes you from behind and then pretends to be innocent.

KIRBY'S NOSE CONTACT

I decided to look closer at the nose contact of a dog that I was taking care of at the time. His name was Kirby. I had noticed that he often used nose contact with me.

When did he do this? That was the first question I wanted to have answered. Was it while we were taking a walk, or "roaming", just like the wolves? Or did it happen on other occasions? I also wanted to see how he did it.

The pattern was very clear. Kirby used nose contact when he seemed to feel an increased need for bonding or closeness: when it was important for him to have direct contact with me, and when he wanted me to be prepared for some kind of communication.

The walks: Normally the number of nose contacts was sparse during our walks. In the beginning, when Kirby was full of energy, it was rather me who had to seek contact with him. As long as we followed familiar roads and paths, nose contact did not happen often. However, when we were approaching crossroads where we sometimes went one way or the other, the nose contact started again.

The same thing happened quite often when we took walks in new areas and if nothing in particular caught Kirby's attention. It happened especially when we walked slowly and the weather was hot. I remember several occasions when he stopped and waited in the shade and then ran to catch up with me. The moment he reached me, Kirby initiated nose contact with me.

The dinner table and the couch in front of the TV: The highest frequency of nose contact took place at the dinner table and at the couch in front of the TV – especially if there was something edible in sight, but also without that. Then Kirby would come up to me and touch me with his nose several times. It is interesting to note that his contact-seeking would have started earlier, while food was being prepared and being served.

In addition to nose contact, I noticed that his glances were frequent. Both the body contact and glances came from all sides. Kirby could be behind me or by my side when he made contact or looked at me. I had to make an effort to study him from the corner of my eye without him noticing that I was observing him.

The interesting thing is that immediately after contact he always took a step back and looked away. This is something that most dog owners have recognized. You feel the nose touch; perhaps even with a nudge as though the dog wants to be petted. But if you actually pet the dog, they seem to ignore it.

Another interesting thing is that most contact was aimed at the hands and arms. Perhaps those places mean something special to a dog. After all, we use our hands and arms all the time when having body contact with our animals.

Your dog will defend you

If you are threatened by anyone, you can count on your dog's support. It will either attack the threatening person or at least disturb the culprit with excessive barking.

It is a deep canine instinct to defend other members of the pack. This has been proven over and over again. Even the nicest dog may suddenly turn into a ferocious beast if its owner is threatened or harassed. But its

As long as its owner is lying down, the dog will be more alert and try to protect him. (Photo: Shutterstock)

protection goes far beyond that. If a dog feels that you are vulnerable in some way it will be more alert and watch over you. This happens for instance when you lie down, as in the following true story.

It was a lovely and relaxed summer's day. A client of mine was sunbathing in a beach chair in the garden with his dog resting in the shade by his side. They were both dozing off, enjoying the day. Suddenly the man heard a noise and looked up. The neighbour's teenage son was approach-

ing. He was one of the dog's favourite people and the two of them used to play and have fun on the lawn. But the dog seemed suddenly to be unable to see him clearly, because he started to growl! Did he not recognize the neighbour's child? This was apparently not the case. The dog's growls grew louder the closer the boy got. My client told his dog to be quiet and uttered the boy's name with a happy, friendly voice. But nothing seemed to calm his dog.

My client wondered whether his dog had gone totally crazy. He was shouting and trying to silence his dog, but it had no effect. The boy stopped and looked puzzled. He hesitated because of the strange message from the dog he thought was his friend. But the growling did not stop. "Something must be really wrong here," my client thought. He sat up to tell the dog to calm down and be nice and quiet. But before he had a chance, the dog stopped and started wagging his tail. The man was dumbfounded. The dog had been a wild beast a second ago and now he was best friends with the neighbour's boy again. Had the dog perhaps developed a "Dr Jekyll and Mr Hyde" tendency, or...?

Do not scold the dog

There is no point in scolding or trying to silence a dog when it acts in a protective manner such as the one described in the story above. This will only cause the dog to be even more alert and protective. What you should do is simply ask the person lying down to sit up. If he or she cannot do that for some reason, use a treat to entice the dog to leave the room. Above all, do not get angry with the dog. It is only doing its instinctive duty.

A DOG PROTECTS THE VULNERABLE

No, the dog did not lose his mind. He acted quite normally, for a dog. The situation is relatively common, and a dog's protective behaviour can be directed at family members as well as acquaintances and strangers. The dog's reaction has to do with its fantastic innate need to protect injured or temporarily weakened comrades.

The same behaviour can be observed among other group-living animals. When I was a boy, I saw this behaviour among the cattle in a farmer's pasture. One of the cows was in pain, and had been put back in the field after surgery. Another cow stayed close to her at all times and was fending off anyone who came too close to her injured friend. I have heard about similar behaviour in other species, for instance elephants, but except from the observation in my childhood I have personally only seen it with dogs.

Back in those days, when my practice included telephone consultations, dog owners used to call me and ask for advice regarding their dog's growling and protective behaviour around someone lying down. It could be a sleeping person, someone sick in bed, or someone just lying down to sunbathe.

Typically, the dog stops the protective behaviour immediately if the person he wants to defend sits or stands up. In the dog's eyes, we are vulnerable only when we lie down. If we stand up, we can defend ourselves.

Your dog stops fights in the family

Dogs want their family, or "pack", to be calm and harmonious. Disagreement within such a close-knit group as a wolf pack could lessen its chance of success in hunting and defence, and thereby threaten everyone's survival.

Dogs seem to have inherited this need for peace in the group, and they usually intervene when they notice a potential risk of friends falling out. On numerous occasions, I have seen how dogs intervene when two other dogs stand rigidly face to face, prepared to start fighting any second.

A Border Collie saw two of his friends standing like this, ready to fight, with deep low growls coming from their snarling lips. Suddenly, the Border Collie started running like a whirling dervish around the two combatants. This furious circling around the two disagreeing dogs calmed them down, and the situation was resolved without a fight. In fact, who can fight when you have somebody running like crazy around you?

On another occasion, I saw a similar situation with two angry dogs, and an older female German Shepherd noticed it. She took off with a flying start and ran straight in between the two, so that they bounced away from each other. That solved the disagreement.

Dogs are guardian angels

Dogs look after their loved ones in many ways. They have warned parents when a baby has had difficulties breathing or has been sleeping in the wrong position. In one incident, a small Terrier came running down the stairs and into the kitchen while barking agitatedly. The mother realized that something was wrong because the dog was acting so crazy. She stopped cooking and asked, "What's wrong?" The Terrier then turned around and ran, leading her upstairs to the nursery. Her newborn daughter lay in her crib and was already blue in the face. The infant was choking to death! However, thanks to the dog her life was saved.

Think about the number of times dogs jump up at their owners when they hug or dance. It is not out of "jealousy", which is a common misinterpretation. The dog sees that mum and dad are standing close to each other and interprets it as a prelude to

People hug each other to express affection, but dogs cannot understand this. To them hugs are a kind of threat. (Photo: Shutterstock)

a fight. It responds to a canine instinct and wants to separate them in order to restore peace within the pack.

An important part of the picture, which leads the dog to regard the situation as a risk, is the fact that the two people stand too close. Closeness and body contact are powerful concepts for dogs, and they cause reactions. That is the reason why dogs growl, turn away or look submissive when being hugged by someone, because it feels threatening. Dogs and hugs do not go together at all.

Dogs can learn to warn their family about a fire. (Photo: Shutterstock)

I always feel sorry for any dog at a dog show when the judge announces that it has won first prize and the overjoyed dog owner gives the dog a big hug. The owner does not see the dog's face, but I do. And the dog looks very unhappy, with the corners of its mouth drawn back, its chin held high and its ears folded back. All these are clear signs of submission, as if the dog wants to say, "I am sorry. I will try not to win again."

Alarm! Alarm!

There are many incidents in which animals have warned their owners about a fire. Here is a true story ...

In the middle of the night, a faint smell is slowly spreading through the house. Noticeable and yet not quite detectible, it is the anaesthetizing, dangerous carbon monoxide, a precursor to smoke and fire.

The old cables have short-circuited, the amber light is growing, and suddenly a flame bursts out in the wooden wall. A greyish-brown smoke slowly rises towards the top floor where the family is sleeping. It will not be long before their escape route down the stairs is blocked ...

A whimpering from their dog quickly changes into an anxious whining. Short quiet barks soon turn into louder ones and then the dog runs upstairs and into the master bedroom, where the dog manages to wake up the parents. They immediately understand the situation and act quickly. They have time to run outside and save themselves and their newborn baby.

The year was 1965. The dog's name was Pia. She was a five-year-old Boxer cross. A couple of weeks earlier she had been adopted by this family and given a chance for a new life. Nobody else had wanted to adopt her. At the time, I was head of the Swedish Dog Protection's dog pound in Stockholm. I was begging our visitors looking for a pet to adopt Pia. She was an older dog and, to be honest, not very good looking. This family had, after some hesitation, decided to take her for a trial period.

Pia became a heroine and what happened that night became a full-page story in the Swedish daily newspaper "Expressen". There was no more talk about a trial period and it did not matter that Pia was an older dog. She stayed with the family for the rest of her life.

After this incident, I often wondered why dogs are able to wake up their owners when a fire starts. However, not all dogs do this. Firefighters told me that the most common outcome is that pets die in the fire together with their families. It was not until many years later that I began understanding the mechanism that underlies why dogs react to smoke and fire and alert their owners. I also realized that if dogs are trained you can drastically increase the chances for all dogs to warn their families in case of fire.

A SLOW START

I developed a training method that worked well and presented it to my dog training students in 1985. However, they were hesitant.

It was something completely new; and, in addition, this new method involved smoke and fire. They did not really buy into this idea, and after trying a few times I gave up.

Ten years later, I was living in Ojai, California, and a dog trainer asked me whether I had any suggestions for a new type of dog training that she could add to her classes. She was so fed up with "all the usual stuff", which was mostly teaching obedience training for young dogs. I told her about the smoke alarm training and she immediately became excited.

I demonstrated the smoke alarm training method and we started working. The first trained dog was a two-year-old Border Terrier. Then came Zippy, a four-year-old crossbreed. Interest in smoke alarm training spread, and courses were held in Sweden and several other countries.

Today, I get reports from a number of countries where trained dogs have been able to warn their families when a real fire has started. I would like to mention Nero, a black Labrador living in Germany. One day, he came running to his owner in the kitchen and barked like crazy. The woman understood that something was wrong, and followed Nero when he ran back into the living room. There, she saw it immediately. A burning candle had been placed on a bookshelf and the heat from the flame was scorching the shelf above. It could have turned into a dangerous fire if the dog had not been trained to alert his owner to smoke. Nero's story was covered in newspaper articles in Germany.

I will never forget the little Australian Shepherd Ozzy. His owner took one of my Smoke Alarm Training courses for dog trainers. Ozzy was a puppy, three and a half months old. During the course, he was just watching the other dogs being trained. Ozzy and his owner Marie walked around and played with the smoke alarm training. One day, when Ozzy was one year old, he came running into Marie's bedroom, visibly upset. As a dog psychologist, Marie understood that something was wrong.

She followed the dog when he ran outside, where she saw smoke at the pump house attached to the house. The electrical system had short-circuited and a real fire could have started at any moment. It threatened to spread to the house where they lived. However, thanks to the dog this never happened. I was impressed to find out that Ozzy in later years actually taught the family's new dogs to alert their owners to smoke and fire. They learnt it only from him – with no other training!

Dogs can differentiate between smoke coming from a cosy fire in the fireplace and smoke that indicates a threatening fire. (Photo: Shutterstock)

LONG BEFORE THE ELECTRONIC FIRE ALARM

Dogs can alert people at least one minute before electronic fire alarms go off. This does not mean that you can disregard the latter: of course they should be installed in all homes. However, because of dogs' ability to react so swiftly to smoke and fire, the smoke alarm training method has received a very positive response from fire department authorities. Lately, insurance companies have also shown an interest in this kind of training.

While an electronic fire alarm only reacts to a certain amount of actual smoke in the same room, a dog detects and reacts to very small amounts, even in other rooms. In one experiment, the electronic fire alarm sounded five minutes after the dog's alert! In fact, we actually had to move the fire alarm closer to the smoke first ...

You might think that trained dogs would react to cigarette smoke, as well as to smoke from a fireplace, but they do not. They just seem to know when we are in control of a situation, for instance making a cosy fire in the fireplace. On the other hand, if we are sleeping or busy away from where the rising smoke is located, they react immediately.

Dogs make us feel good!

With their finely tuned antennas, dogs seem to be able to sense our every mood. If you are happy, then your dog is happy. If you are sad, no one is better at comforting you. Although dogs can be sad, they do not cry tears like us. Somehow, they seem to understand when someone is sad or have tears running down their cheeks. Do dogs have a sixth sense or are they simply very sensitive to how we feel? We might never get an answer to this question, but sometimes I wonder...

HEALTHCARE

Society is saving a lot of money thanks to dogs, because they make us feel good and keep us healthy. Dogs give us exercise, company, a feeling of safety and they become someone who needs us. The fact that someone needs you is considered a very important thing in anybody's life. We all need to feel needed and to have someone to care for, someone to live for.

At an old people's home in Connecticut, USA, half of the patients were given a flowerpot to nurture and water (21). The nurses also listened more to the views and wishes of those patients. The other half also got a flowerpot, but it was taken care of by the personnel, who did not pay special attention to the old people's wishes or views. After a few years, the death rate was half as high in the first group compared with the one where the flowers were taken care of by others.

Today we know that dogs provide a feeling of being needed, which is so important. It is true for young and older children, teenagers, adults and old people – everybody feels good in the company of dogs. In addition, if you feel good in your soul you keep physically healthy.

Dogs can encourage children to practise reading.
(Photo: Shutterstock)

It has been noticed that dogs can lower blood pressure in humans – just by being in the room. This is said with a slight reservation, because the dogs need to be really well behaved. Stressed, barking and angry dogs, on the other hand, will probably raise the blood pressure of most people.

When you touch a dog's fur, your pulse slows down, your blood pressure decreases and the hormone oxytocin, which instils a feeling of peace, is released in your brain.

CHILDREN AND DOGS

Studies have shown that children who grow up with dogs in the home end up with better social competence in later life. They are better at understanding and conveying non-verbal communication, that is, body language in its various forms. Those children also grow up with more self-confidence and a more positive outlook towards other people. They are often more open and spontaneous and it is easier for them to express what they feel.

The company of a pet brings a feeling of safety. This can be a big plus in modern society, where often both parents are working and their offspring spend their time at day care. Research on dog–child companionship has shown that children who grow up with pets in the home are less likely to continue sucking their thumbs (22).

Today there are trained "trauma dogs" in Sweden. Katja Thorman initiated this training some years ago. She runs a centre with helper dogs for owners with special needs and service dogs (37). Thorman had the idea that children who had been involved in an accident may find comfort and support in a dog if it was taken right to the scene of the accident. This therapy has proven to give very good results.

Dogs have been shown to be of special value in relation to children's schoolwork. The British journalist Kay White started a club for children with reading and writing difficulties (39). The central figure in the club was her female Boxer, Pixie. White let the children get friendly with the dog at a special event. Then they were encouraged to write letters to the dog, who in turn "responded" to their letters. In this way the children got extra practice in reading and writing, but it also developed into something much more. In their letters, the children dared to share their innermost thoughts and feelings with Pixie, and it was often things they did not dare to talk about with their parents or other adults adults. It could even be about serious matters such as abuse and problems at home.

Dogs have also been brought in as "schoolwork helpers", where a child reads stories to the dog. This method has by now been practised in many countries and it has shown that children find it easier to practise reading in this way, rather than reading to an adult.

Dogs are fantastic!

- Dog owners are happier
- Dog owners are healthier
- Dog owners feel better psychologically
- Dogs are the best tool in neighbourhood watch, walking around with their owners
- Children learn responsibility and respect from dogs and develop social skills
- Dogs provide companionship and security to older people
- Companion dogs visit institutions

Dogs do this:

- Help children with special needs (reading stimulation, helping autistic children, etc.)
- Help the disabled (guide dogs for the blind, service and hearing dogs)
- Help detect hidden mines for the military
- Help police and customs
- Find lost and drowned people
- Find the injured in ruins
- Find gas leaks
- Find mould in electrical and telephone poles
- Seek and mark mould in buildings
- Alert people when there is a fire (especially after smoke alarm training)
- Help hunters find game in the wild
- Find injured game in the wild
- Help farmers to herd and move cattle

Dogs really have earned a right to be treated well and with love.

UNDERSTANDING YOUR DOG

Dogs have feelings and thoughts – and they understand much more than you think. Even if a dog does not understand all of the words you are saying, it listens very attentively. A dog is always honest and straightforward regarding feelings. Dogs are intelligent and they follow the social rules set up in ancient times. They do not like stressful situations and they hate to be caged in small spaces. They depend on your care and knowledge as well as your love and understanding.

The fact that dogs have a rich and developed emotional life is becoming clearer after recent research in this field. Consequently, they possess the entire register of emotions from joy to sorrow, from excitement to sadness, from suffering to playfulness, from anguish to aggression. Furthermore, they are intelligent and have a talent for learning. Moreover, if we just allow them to develop their abilities they can achieve astonishing things.

Ancient instincts are blended with a dog's modern talents. It is rare that a dog will hurt people or other dogs. Those who inflict damage on others are usually not following the unwritten rules hidden in every dog's genes. Their behaviour is in many cases caused by sickness or pain, or

(Photo: Maurer)

it occurs because the individual has been exposed to extreme stress.

Dogs have instinctive rules regarding how to meet and greet. The ceremony consists of a number of rituals, all of which are meant to neutralize any possible animosity. If we were as polite towards dogs as they expect us to be, we would never see dogs being shy when meeting strangers.

Do dogs understand everything we say?

"He understands everything I say," dog owners often say about their beloved pet. But does the dog really understand everything we say? Can it understand the words we use, and how important is the tone of voice here?

The dog's ability to understand the meaning of words has been researched thoroughly. Dogs can learn the meaning of around two hundred words. Some dogs have been trained to learn even more. They have learned the words by association, which means that dogs have learned to associate one word, for instance "ball", with the ball as an object. This is on the same level as a two-year-old child.

To understand a word is another story. This means that an individual knows the meaning of the word. If I say "good dog", then the dog associates the words with my joy, some petting and often a treat. It understands what the words are associated with, not what they really mean. I

If a dog tilts its head, it may be listening attentively, but that does not mean that it really understands what is said. (Photo: Maurer)

could just as well sound encouraging when I say "bad, ugly dog" and get the same reaction from the dog.

Tone of voice is probably the most important factor. Dogs are sensitive to our tone of voice. This becomes apparent when we try saying a word in different ways, regardless of the meaning of the word. If you sound harsh the dog will look scared or submissive, if you sound happy then it will be happy, if you pity the dog it will look pitiful regardless of the meaning of the word.

You might say, "But I can see that he understands me. It shows by the way he pricks up his ears and the alertness of his eyes and the way he tilts his head when I speak to him." Yes, naturally, but that does not mean that he understands what you are talking about. What you see is a dog that is listening and perhaps waiting for words that it can recognize and expects to hear, such as "dinner", "go for a walk", "mummy", "daddy" and other words it is used to hearing.

We can easily ascertain that dogs do not understand everything we say, but that they listen to our tone of voice as well as waiting to hear familiar words.

PERCEPTION OF TIME

Dogs do not know the difference between past and future tenses. They hear everything as "now". So if you say, "Mummy will be here soon," your dog will run to the door to greet her. The dog does not know the meaning of "soon", it only hears "Mummy is coming."

I have heard many dog owners say to their dog after a walk: "That was such a nice walk, wasn't it?" The dog only recognizes the word "walk", and does not connect that with the walk they just have had.

Therefore, it is important to think "now" when you talk to your dog and avoid using other time references. Do not use words such as "later" and "soon".

You could say that this limitation in time perception in dogs is a good thing. They live in the here and now. They do not regret yesterday and do not worry about tomorrow. What a nice philosophy to live by! We have a lot to learn from dogs.

NEGATIONS

Dogs cannot understand negations, such as the word "not", used in connection with other words. If you say, "do not jump", the dog might possibly understand the word "jump", but not that you mean that it should not jump. It is the same with all negative terms. It is better to use single words that they understand, such as "no". However, the problem is that few dogs have learned the meaning of the word "no"; they react to your angry tone of voice. Not a good thing ...

Are dogs defiant?

People interpret and explain dog behaviour on the basis of their personal knowledge, and sometimes, unfortunately, according to what suits them and their purpose.

Someone might happen to hurt a dog, perhaps when cutting its nails, grooming it or during a medical treatment. When the dog then yelps, the person then might say that the dog is being "over sensitive" or "just acting silly". Saying this makes the person look innocent and all the blame is put on the dog.

It is not unusual for the same thing to happen when a dog is "disobedient" when given a command. Then the dog might be called stupid, because it does not seem to understand. In situations like these, it seems as though you have a right to be angry, especially if you perceive the dog to be "defiant" or "obstinate". Once again, the blame is unfairly put on the dog and not the person.

These interpretations are wrong and based on ignorance. You are using the power of the word to put yourself in a better light and blame everything on the dog. It is time for us to see through this "power language", fight it, and try to get rid of it once and for all.

So, if someone hurts a dog and makes it sound as though it was the dog's own fault, you should protest immediately and make clear that it is the person who should be blamed, not the dog.

DOGS ARE HONEST

Dogs are always straightforward and show their feelings. They are not defiant, because that would mean a conscious decision to protest against something. Rather, they could be unmotivated, scared or blocked by something. They are not obstinate or bloody minded – that would need a human brain. They experience discomfort, are stressed or avoid the situation at hand for another reason.

Dogs are not wimps – they protest or try to get away because they feel fear, pain or anxiety around a certain person or situation. If a dog whines and wants to run away from the veterinarian or a person cutting its nails, or when it is being groomed or when a trainer is too rough, it is not because it is a "coward". It is because the dog is experiencing anxiety.

People that rationalize, gloss over or dismiss anxiety and apparent discomfort in dogs are often lacking in empathy. Perhaps it is because those people have been working with dogs for too many years and have lost their empathy, perhaps they belong to the "harsher" school of training, are ignorant about ethology and psychology or just do not have enough patience with what they are doing.

> ### It is never the dog's fault
>
> It does not matter how you look at the facts. It is never the dog's fault if it displays any form of discomfort. The person behind the discomfort is always to blame. As a dog owner, it is your responsibility to protect your dog and to make sure it is never unnecessarily exposed to scary or painful experiences.
>
> Please remember:
> A dog is not defiant, obstinate, pigheaded, bloody-minded, stupid, ridiculous, namby-pamby, coward, daft, foolish, wimpy, nonchalant, ignorant, faking or acting silly on purpose.

No matter how bored they are, dogs never complain. (Photo: Shutterstock)

Dogs do not complain

When I was a child there was a Dachshund living in our neighbourhood. She was so fat that she could hardly walk. When she was taken out, it was just to do her business, quick and near the front door. Then back inside. She never got any exercise.

I felt so sorry for her, but there was no way I could influence the dog's owners. I was only six years old. But the memory stayed with me – such a wasted life just because of her owner's indolence and lack of empathy and understanding.

Unfortunately, many dogs that live poor lives like that, with short walks, or no walks at all or perhaps even tied to a short rope by the door or a kennel.

Old people seldom complain. They sit there in their chairs or lie in bed and accept being forgotten by their loved ones. They have given up. They do not want to be of any trouble and do not want to complain. Luckily, there are exceptions.

There is no excuse

To get a puppy and then let it slide into some kind of zero exis- tence, and refrain from giving it proper walks, exercise and other daily care and attention is highly irresponsible and unethical. It is degrading and represents an all-time low in human behaviour.

With dogs, there are no exceptions. They never complain, no matter how badly they are treated, or how forgotten and ignored they are. Just like the Dachshund from my childhood. She was really happy and thankfully wagged her tail when she received some attention. The rest of the time, she was just lying still in her bed.

Many dogs end up with severe behav- ioural problems when they are mistreated; the sad result is often that they will be treated even more badly. The owners do not realise that the dog's behavioural prob- lems are a symptom of how they handle it.

Dogs have an egocentric worldview

Imagine that you are walking your dog and you encounter a patch of ice on the ground. You slip and stumble and the dog jumps away in fear until stopped by the length of its leash. This is a completely natural reac- tion, but what happens next does not at all seem logical at first glance. The dog hunch- es down in fear, its ears folded back, its neck lowered, its chin raised and its tail between its legs. These are all submission signals!

It looks as though the dog is afraid of you, and thinks that you are going to at- tack it for no reason. And all you did was stumble.

DO NOT COMFORT

Dogs are egocentric, just like other animals. Their ego is the centre of their world and everyone around has a more or less impor- tant function. That is completely natural for animals, including humans, and quite understandable.

This means that a dog reacts to what is happening around it from "an egocentric perspective". Consequently, a dog thinks that every action nearby is directed towards it, even if this is not the case. When you slip and stumble on that ice patch and wave your arms and shout, your dog will perceive that behaviour as an attack.

The dog is afraid because it cannot find any reason for your attack. It cannot under- stand that you just slipped by accident. So if you then begin to comfort the dog it will only make it feel more uncomfortable and show even more submissive behaviour.

Your first action after stumbling therefore should be directed away from the dog. Per- haps you could dance a few steps, shout

out in joy and clearly demonstrate that you do not see the dog as part of what just happened. At best, the dog then may think that you attacked something else. On the other hand, if the dog is clever, it will believe that you just had one of those silly outbursts of joy that you seem to have on occasion.

It is important to understand that dogs are self-centred. Then you will also be able to stop a dog from being unnecessarily frightened and submissive. If there are many upsetting incidents, such as slips and stumbles, a dog may in time lose self-esteem and the ability to take the initiative. This happens with dogs that are punished and corrected often. You could compare it to the way you handle small, upsetting everyday situations.

EVERYTHING YOU DO CAN BE MISINTERPRETED

It's not just sudden movements and small accidents that may lead a dog to believe that an action is aimedz at itself.If you happen to step on a paw or if the dog gets hurt when you are near-by, you will get the same reaction. At every such incident you should express a little joy or dance a few steps to distract the dog.

What neighbours and other people think about you does not really matter. People without pets will certainly think you are a bit weird, but that is just part of being a dog owner.

I had a case involving a Border Collie that ran away to hide whenever a soccer game was on TV. The owners could not understand why he reacted this way. I asked if the man was a sports fan, and he was. When watching a game, he became so involved that he would scream and yell. That was the answer! The dog did not understand that the TV programme made his master so upset. Instead, he thought that he was angry with him.

Do not quarrel!

Something you might seldom think of is the effect of conflicts in the home. Two people have a disagreement and argue. What they do not notice in their agitated state is that the dog is scared by the loud and bitter exchange of words. The dog will of course believe that it is the one getting a real scolding. It is obvious if you look at its body language. Tail stuck between its legs, ears pushed back, lowered body posture and worried eyes.

If you have a dog, you should not argue in its presence. Take a cold shower or go somewhere else to argue. By that time, you might even have forgotten what all the fuss was about ...

If they are being motivated and rewarded, dogs learn as fast as humans. (Photo: Shutterstock)

Dogs are intelligent and emotional beings

Dogs are intelligent animals. Their capacity for learning is just as high as that of human beings, even if they are not able to remember as much. The time they take to learn is also the same, especially if they learn by operant conditioning, which means that they are being motivated and have to use their brains to figure out what to do in order to get the reward.

If, for instance, you wish to use the operant learning model to teach your dog to bark on command, show it a treat or a toy. The dog will then try various behaviours until the correct one is rewarded with the treat or a toy. Perhaps it will lie down or jump up on you, sit down or lift a paw. While trying all of these things it might give out a little bark, and then immediately it gets a reward. This way the dog quickly understands that it is the bark you want when you say, "bark".

IS THE TEACHER OR THE PUPIL RESPONSIBLE?

Dogs seem to have a hard time learning not to do things such as barking at other dogs or chasing after joggers or other animals. This is not because they lack the ability to learn, but because dog owners do not know how to train them. If you can motivate your dog and train it correctly, then you will have quick and lasting results. Unfortunately, many often try to punish the dog when it does something wrong, which will only change its behaviour temporarily.

With correct training, your dog will be quiet when you ask it to be and it will not run after joggers or other "prey". Instead, it will come and "report" to you when it has seen something exciting. This happened to Irene, one of my dog psychology students. She lived in a cottage in a wooded area. Her dog chased after deer whenever she had the chance. Irene began training her with a clicker. Every time the dog spotted a deer, which was almost daily, she heard a clicker sound that meant "Good, girl! You saw a deer! Here's a treat". After two weeks, when the dog was running free, suddenly a deer appeared. The dog stopped dead, seemingly confused, as if she was trying to say, "I have seen a deer! Click and give me a treat!"

DIFFERENT PARTS OF THE BRAIN

The brain can be divided into two parts. One is involved with cognitive functions such as thoughts, calculations and learning.

These cognitive processes occur in the prefrontal cortex, a younger part of the brain. The other part processes emotions created in the deeper areas of the brain, in the so-called limbic system. This area regulates emotions and memory. Here you will find small areas on each side, called the amygdala. Research has shown that they perform a primary role in the processing of a dog's emotional reaction. When these areas are triggered by electrical impulses, the result is strong emotional outbursts.

Dogs are not as well equipped as humans when it comes to thought processes. Their brains are just not as big as ours. Nevertheless, they do have a well-developed emotional system and this makes them more responsive to feelings rather than cognitive reactions. However, this does not mean that they lack cognitive abilities – on the contrary. As mentioned earlier, they have a marvellous ability to evaluate, learn, figure out and think.

SMART SPECIALISTS

Dogs are intelligent, especially in particular fields. They are specialists in certain areas. This ability is perhaps easier to understand when we consider their heritage from the wolf.

Our domestic dogs are in many ways just like their ancestors, despite the fact that there are several thousands of years of evolution between them. Different breeds are predisposed to perform different behaviours. For instance, the Border Collie's herding ability has not removed the "wolf" in the dog. Neither has domestication dampened their strong instinctive canine behaviour.

SOCIAL INTERACTION AND COMMUNICATION

For a pack of wolves to survive in the harsh wilderness its individuals must be able to function well with each other socially. They have to get along, because fights among themselves would have an adverse effect on the whole group. Since the group is normally a family, the individuals are very close-knit. This is a must, because the younger ones are dependent on the older members for successful hunting and survival. Because the elders are socially competent, threats and open aggression are rare.

The interaction in the pack is built on communication. It consists of body signals, facial expressions, sounds, touch and other things in a complex language that every wolf can use to make itself

The members of a wolf pack depend on each other and must get along well. (Photo: Shutterstock)

understood. It works exactly the same for dogs, even though they differ physically from their ancestors after so many years of evolution.

If you study the language of wolves and dogs in all its nuances, you really have to be impressed. Suddenly our human language seems poor. Dogs can share an incredible amount of information, but unfortunately we are not very good at interpreting their signals.

When a dog is displaying "a peace flag" using aggression-inhibiting signals, an excited person often does not seem to understand it. Perhaps the dog has chewed and ruined something in the house because it was bored when the owners were away for too long. Although the dog shows all instinctive signals to stop aggression, the dog owner breaks the unwritten rule to refrain from being angry – and instead punishes the dog. This is very disturbing for the dog.

CARE AND PROTECTION OF PUPPIES

To care for its young is crucial for the survival of any species. Experiments have shown that the "maternal instinct", for example the protection of one's own baby, is the strongest driving force of all. Food, sexual partners and other important things cannot be compared with what a mother is prepared to sacrifice in order to protect her offspring.

This instinct can also be observed in dogs and it will be expressed in many different ways. For a dog, our children are puppies and therefore included in their protective

behaviour. All parents who have taken a walk with a baby stroller and their dog have probably seen how the dog discreetly places itself between the stroller and any stranger who tries to take a peek at the baby.

The case of an 11-year old Pekinese female is a strong illustration of the above. When the ower, a young mother, came home from the maternity ward with her little newborn baby, her Pekinese dog was upset and barked. Neighbours and a number of other "experts" had previously warned her that the dog could hurt the newborn, so the dog's reaction scared the young mother.

She was worried and called me to ask if she had to put the dog to sleep. I asked when the dog was last in heat, which was two months previously. I instantly understood what was going on and told her to sit down on the floor with the baby on one arm and hold the phone with the other hand. The dog came up to her. With a trembling voice, she told me that the dog started to lick and clean the baby. I explained that the dog saw the baby asa new member of the family and that she wanted to help take care of the baby. The little Pekinese was after all also a new mother. She had recently had a false pregnancy.

CARE AND PROTECTION EACH OTHER

As a family is a tight knit group it is obvious that the members care for and protect each other when necessary. This has been proved in many observations of both dogs and wolves, although most studies, for obvious reasons, have been carried out on dogs. Dogs are part of our daily lives, and there are more opportunities to study their relationship with us.

Expression of care in groups of dogs is mostly done with the tongue and it is normal for dogs in a family to "clean" each other as well as us. If we have a wound the dog seems to want to lick and "clean" it. This is often something that we do not think is appropriate. The truth is that a dog's mouth is considered cleaner than a human being's.

As mentioned earlier, dogs will protect a person lying down, even if he or she is just sunbathing or relaxing in bed. They also protect us against threatening people, angry dogs and more. In addition, they guard and protect our home – one of the reasons why people get a dog. They also seem to feel that they have to protectour car.

SYNCHRONIZATION

With animals that have evolved to an intelligent specialization, you have to include the ability of a group to synchronize their actions with each other. It is easy to see the advantages if wolves in a pack coordinate their behaviour. At a given time, they all have an equal amount of energy. They all rest at the same timeand they all are active at the same time, which makes them a perfect-ly coodinated team equal to a military platoon. Our domestic dogs still show this kind of behaviour.

COOPERATION

Another excellent talent, shared by both wolves and dogs, is the ability to work together. Unfortunately, there is not much research in this field (20). Wolves work together during a hunt, chiefly when going after big game such as moose or an American bison. During the attack, they maintain close eye contact with each other. They also seem to know their position in this organized operation, so that one wolf will disturb the animal from behind, another circles around, and others attack from both flanks and the front.

There is a story of a wolf pack in Canada that drove their prey towards fallen power lines. An abandoned power plant lay within their territory and poles had fallen and lay scattered on the ground. The wolves drove the animals slowly but surely, from behind and each side, towards these poles and lines. When they got closer to the area, the wolves sped up the chase and gave the animals no time to discover the power lines until they were entangled and stuck in them.

Similar examples of dogs cooperating are when they are hunting and herding, that is to say in all situations where dogs must work together with their owners. Dogs work together with hunters in various ways. Some are trained to find and "stand" by the prey. Others chase the animals towards the hunter. Dogs can herd sheep or cattle in a certain direction or to a specific location. Police dogs, rescue dogs, service dogs, therapy dogs and many

Sheepdogs can herd animals in a certain direction and cooperate closely with the shepherd. (Photo: Shutterstock)

other specially trained dogs also perform important tasks with their owners.

INTERCEPT AND CALCULATE ANGLES

Another intelligent behaviour observed in wolves and dogs is the ability to intercept. During the hunt it is of course crucial that they can intercept an animal's flight path. That will save energy for the hunter and tire the prey.

I have observed this ability in so many dogs, and every time it impresses me. I can throw a ball against the wall at any angle and watch how the dog knows exactly at what angle the ball will bounce back, and catch it there. I have carried out this experiment many times and always with the same result. Dogs really know how to calculate angles and intercept objects in motion.

During one period I tried an experiment to see whether horses and cows had the same ability. I walked past a field with horses and cows every day and gave them a treat such as bread or carrots. After a few days they learned that I always had something for them, and when they spotted me they came up to the fence. They saw me walking in the direction of where the fence ended. But could they figure out where they should meet me? A dog would have calculated where I would end up. However, these horses and cows could not do it. They were focused on me the entire time and did not have the ability to calculate the angle at which I walked and intercept me. Perhaps this is something only predators can do.

TAKING A DETOUR

I did a number of tests on dogs' ability to solve detour problems. One test was to let a dog into a fenced field while the owner was standing outside, away from the gate. The owner then called for the dog by the fence, but further away from the gate, so that the dog could not reach them. It did not take long for the dogs in this test to understand that they needed to leave that area and run to the gate to get out of the field and join their owner.

Dogs know how to calculate angles and intercept an object such as a ball in motion. (Photo: Shutterstock)

I tested another situation, which I am sure many dog owners are familiar with, in which the dog ends up on the other side of a tree or a post and the leash stops the dog from going forward. If you stand still, most dogs will solve the problem themselves by going back to the right side of the tree or the post.

PERCEPTION OF WORDS

As mentioned earlier, a dog does not understand everything we say but listens more to our tone of voice. Despite this, a dog can learn the meaning of around two hundred words. If you really focus on teaching dogs to understand words, you can increase their vocabulary even more.

A Border Collie female named Chaser is famous for knowing the difference between more than a thousand words! Her owner, professor of psychology John Pilley in South Carolina, USA, has systematically trained her ability.

You might think your dog is very clever and understands everything you say. If so, perhaps you should take a moment to reflect on whether or not you are playing on the dog's feelings, and that is the response you see in the dog's eager and expectant look. The dog waits for words and other signals which can trigger various emotions. For example "Shall we take a walk?" or "Shall we play?" incites joy, while "Bye, bye! I will be back soon" evokes discomfort. The dog often does not understand the meaning of the word, but sees it as a "signal".

Dogs have emotions!

Above all, we need to realize that dogs are emotional beings. Therefore, it is important that dogs be given a chance to feel motivated. Motivation is crucial for learning.

To meet and greet – dogs are polite

One of the most important things in a dog's social life is how to meet new acquaintances. You can, without exaggeration, say that dogs are among the most polite animals in the world, and they are very particular in their social interaction.

MEETING CALMLY

A dog should not run straight towards another dog. This can be misinterpreted as an attack if it is a strange dog approaching at high speed. The dog who feels threatened might then bite and even hurt the rude stranger.

Puppies have a hard time controlling themselves. They often speed off when they see another dog. Although they are young, they seem to know what to do. Right before they reach the other dog they slow down, make

Sniffing each other around the nose is part of the greeting ritual. (Photo: Shutterstock)

themselves small, hunch down or even lie down, thus giving a clear signal that all they want to do is play.

Young dogs also have a problem holding back, but they have another technique to signal that they are not attacking. They take aim at a point next to the dog they want to run to, as if they are just passing. In doing this, the message is clear: they just want to say hello and perhaps play a little.

Adult dogs usually use speed to convey the same message when running towards another dog. The nearer they come, the slower they move. They also wag their tails. These signals send a clear message of peaceful intent.

GREETING NICELY

When the approaching dog arrives, several greeting rituals begin. The puppy licks the corner of the other dog's mouth, makes itself small, perhaps rolling on its back, quickly wagging its tail and making little tempting jumps as an invitation to play.

The youngster normally does not show as many submissive signals as the puppy when greeting other dogs, but it wags its tail just as much, backs up and takes little jumps forwards and to the side as an invitation to play. Sometimes it can pick up a stick and run around with it to invite the other dog to chase after it.

The adult dog seldom invites play. To start the greeting ritual is more important. Both dogs first sniff each other around the nose, then around the ears and throat. There are no particular smells around these parts, so this is probably just to show how careful and polite they are, and that they are following the proper rituals. If none of them has shown any discomfort by then, they carefully approach the hind end. The most important scents are there, and they reveal plenty about the other individual. If both dogs now decide that they like each other, they can start playing. They are a little careful at first, just to make sure that they are both friendly, and keep to the unwritten rules of friendship.

If one dog is too quick in sniffing the other's backside, as sometimes happens if a young dog is enthusiastic, it might get an immediate sharp correction. Often this is done so forcefully that the younger dog flees or drops down on its back like a puppy.

MEETING FRIENDS

When two dogs of the same sex that know each other well have been separated for a time, the reunion can be sensitive. This is also true for dogs living in the same family. Perhaps one of them has been away for a few days at a dog show, or has stayed at the veterinarian hospital, for example.

When they are reunited one of them, often the one that stayed at home, will appear stiff and threatening. If the returning dog does not show strong submission it might be attacked, and a serious fight could result.

The reason for the conflict here is difficult to explain, but it can also be noticed among wolves. It is as though relations have to be tested again when they have been apart. The home territory also seems to be of great importance because the tension does not arise beyond that.

The solution is to let the dogs reunite outside somewhere on neutral ground. Take the dog who has stayed at home out for a walk and then let the two dogs meet on the way. In this case the reunion is usually a moment of joy and play, without any tension. The dogs can then go home together and normally there will be no problem.

MEETING PEOPLE

Meeting rituals and reunions between dogs usually function very well. They seem to know about these things instinctively. Stressed dogs and dogs in pain can be an exception, but even those usually behave well during meetings and reunions.

Unfortunately, the described system does not work so well between dogs and people – even though there is nothing wrong with the dogs' behaviour. All too few people know how to greet dogs in a polite and proper dog manner.

Children often run fast, straight towards a dog. It surprises me every time that, in such a situation, more dogs do not protest sharply. It is important that parents know a little about dogs so that they can tell their children how to behave correctly. Dog owners must also step in and protect their dogs. The easiest way to do this is to stop the child for a moment and then let it give the dog a treat. This usually solves the situation immediately. You have to watch so that the child only pets the dog lightly and does not hug it, which is a clear threat in dog language.

Unfortunately, many adults also do not know or simply ignore dogs' meeting rules. They just walk up to the dog without giving it a chance to sniff them slowly and get familiar with them. The dog needs to do this because human beings do not wag their tails or show any other friendly signals. Many do not even hunch down but stand threateningly or bend over the dog with bared teeth (smiling). Poor dogs! When you think about it, it is strange that they manage as well as they do.

Highly strung dogs are disliked

On occasion, both wild and tame dogs or wolves may start to fight. The most common reason is when they are competing over food, or males are fighting over females when they are in heat. Another reason might be when fast and intense movements have caused disruption of a peace-

ful situation. This could also happen when an over-active dog does not stop playing even after the others have done so.

ADAPTATION IS IMPORTANT

Normally, dogs in a group adapt well to each other. It does not matter whether the dogs belong to the same family, are friends that meet often, or are dogs that meet occasionally. After some initial greeting ceremonies, followed by a moment of fun chasing games, most dogs calm down. When some dogs in the group stop running around and play, the rest of the group follow their example. It is part of the dog's nature to want to synchronize with the rest of the group. This is important in order to function well together. Once upon a time, it increased their success when hunting.

DEVIANT INDIVIDUALS ARE CORRECTED

If a dog fails to coordinate its energy with the rest of the group and continues to run around like crazy and tries to get the others to play, one or several in the group will be irritated. They will growl and bark at the wild one and intercept the individual aggressively. The result is often that the wild one becomes submissive, yelps and leaves the group, as if to say, "What have I done wrong?"

There are over-energetic dogs that do not learn from even the harshest corrections from other dogs. They might get in trouble time after time and often become increasingly irritated by this. Once I saw a Border Collie running free with several other dogs. He was not used to meeting other dogs, so he seemed overjoyed. He quickly greeted a few of them and then started to run wildly around them. The others had not finished their greeting ceremonies and you could see the irritation growing towards the runner. Quite soon, the others began trying to stop him, but he just increased his speed and thought it was a game. Suddenly I saw a couple of dogs focusing on the Border Collie and trying to catch him, but it was not possible. Their irritation grew stronger. The owner of the dog realized what was about to happen and intervened before his dog got into serious trouble.

Stress builds up

Outbursts of strong emotion, such as fear and aggression, always need a period of recuperation. If a dog has been scared or angry it needs some time to regain a sense of calm and balance. This takes longer than you might think.

After a powerful and stressful event that lasts one or two minutes, a dog will need around ten or twenty minutes to recuperate. However, there might be after-effects from the incident for several days. This might be related to

Greeting rituals are often followed by short chasing games. (Photo: Shutterstock)

changes in the neurotransmitters in the brain as well as an increased amount of stress hormones.

NEUROLOGICAL ASPECTS

Thus, the influence of a traumatic experience may be at the level of the brain, often with other functions involved. Increased preparedness can result, caused by visual and auditory memories, an increased sensitivity to sudden stimuli, tension in the muscles and a changed level of alertness. A dog's reaction time is also affected after a traumatic experience. In many individuals, it will be so short that the reaction comes at the same time as the stressful event, for example if the dog hears a sudden bang.

All of this contributes to lowering the dog's threshold for external stimuli. It will also experience everything in a more heightened state than before – even events that previously did not cause any particular reaction. If a dog has been frightened by a sound, for instance, it will be more sensitive to that kind of sound for a long period. If a dog is provoked by another dog and responds with an attack, this will increase its preparedness to attack other dogs for a long time after that. This is especially true if the other dog looks similar to the provoking dog.

STRESS HORMONES

A dog's change in behaviour after a traumatic experience may also be as a result of an increased production of stress hormones such as adrenaline, noradrenaline and cortisol. It is known that such a change takes place after a shock or even after a prolonged period of stress. Levels of cortisol, the "negative stress hormone", increase during and for a long time after training with an electric collar (32).

LONG-LASTING EFFECTS

Consequently, the effects of an aggressive outburst or a frightening experience stay with a dog for a long time. Even if a dog seems to have got over whatever happened, this does not mean that the effect of the experience is really gone from its nervous system. Something that seems to have been forgotten in a couple of minutes has in fact re-programmed the dog's mind and body to be in a state of heightened alert for the next few hours or perhaps even days afterwards.

The effects of a traumatic experience last for a long time, which is illustrated by the fact that we dream about it. People and dogs – and probably all mammals – dream more often and more actively after a powerful experience. In human dreams, the event itself is often remembered. Perhaps it is the same with dogs.

CUMULATIVE EFFECT

Whenever something upsetting happens, and before the effect of the prior incident is completely gone, any event can add to the first trauma. If a dog is scared

A frightening experience stays with a dog for a long time. (Photo: Shutterstock)

by a sudden loud sound, its heightened preparedness for danger probably remains even a couple of hours later. This reaction to the new noise will be stronger than if the dog had had time to recuperate completely from its first scare. The effects accumulate – they add up.

This might explain why many dogs that normally are not frightened easily by a single rocket or firework will be scared and traumatized after the rapid and repeated sounds of multiple fireworks going off. In light of this, we need to understand that fireworks are very risky for dogs, even if they are normally not scared.

The cumulative effect also influences the outcome of mental testing of dogs. If a dog experiences unease during one part of the test, the risk immediately increases that it will react with fear in the next part of the test. Therefore, test results can be beset with errors, and one should not give too much credit to the results of such mental tests.

The cumulative effect in everyday life

When you take a dog for a walk on a leash, you need to stop now and then, perhaps before crossing the street, or to stop the dog from running towards another dog that seems tense. When you begin to walk again, you may notice that your dog is in a hurry and wants to pull forwards.
It is as if the dog's energy builds up when it has to stand still for a moment, and after that, it has an excess of energy. This is a good example for the cumulative effect.

Caged – dogs in small spaces

To shut a dog up in a cage, a car or a pen or to tie a dog up other than temporarily is painful for many reasons. One of them is that this goes against the dog's nature. As ancestors of the wolf for thousands of years, they have the same needs. They are genetically programmed for the best possible chance of survival, and this cannot be removed by domestication, breeding or training.

Dogs have, of course, the same need as all mammals to be able to exercise and move about freely. Good physical condition is necessary for wolves in order to cope with and perform during hunting. It is a major factor in survival. In addition to having a strong fitness base, they need to move around and exercise just as much as athletes who need to keep themselves in top condition.

Denying your dog daily long walks and other physical activity deprives it of a basic need, which is almost as important as food. Too little exercise becomes a stress factor!

DOG CRATES HAVE BECOME POPULAR

Some dog trainers recommend putting the dog in a flight cage, or crate, as a way of house training a puppy, or teaching the dog not to run around in the house and to keep it away from guests. A good trainer does NOT need the use of a cage to achieve all of this ...

Dogs that react to being caged by yelping, barking, howling and digging are often punished so hard for this that they give up and become silent.

A dog in a cage has no power over its situation, no matter how much it tries to change something. Eventually it will resign and sink into a state of helplessness. American scientist and psychologist Martin Seligman, who developed the theory of "learned helplessness", researched this phenomenon. The symptoms are similar to those of depression and many believe that it is the same thing.

Dogs should be fully included in the family life. (Photo: Maurer)

A NEED FOR FRIENDSHIP AND COMPANY

Family, social interaction and emotional bonds between individuals are of great importance to dogs. Many behaviours can be used to strengthen these essential bonds, for instance grooming, play and body contact – all of these behaviours require that you do not exclude your dog from social relationships.

Company and social interaction are two important things for dogs. To leave a dog alone for the entire day while you are working is wrong for such a social animal. Also, excluding your dog from your family's life when you are at home is unnatural and painful for a dog. Therefore, a dog should be able to move around freely in the same rooms as you do, and you should never use a cage.

Ethology teaches us
WHAT MAKES DOGS HAPPY

In this chapter, I will explain the importance of not only love and knowledge but also the ability to feel empathy. Dogs have thoughts and feelings and they understand more than you may think. They are intelligent! A dog is always honest when showing its feelings.

If you feel you have to work on your own "leadership" skills, then you can relax. You are automatically the leader! This chapter explains why a dog sees you as a role model, which can have serious consequences if you misbehave and act in too authoritarian a manner. It is, however, never wrong to give a dog a treat while training. Ethology teaches us that those who argue for a dog training method without the use of force and violence, pulling and shouting, and without too much demand for obedience are definitely right.

Of course, you want your dog to enjoy life with you and your family. It has such a short life and the most important thing is to fill it with joy and activities. That said we also have to ask the big philosophical question: What is a happy life for a dog? Is it if a dog is loved and can do whatever it wants? Is a dog happy when trained to be obedient and well behaved? What is happiness, when seen from an ethological and psychological perspective?

(Photo: Maurer)

Who is a good dog owner?

Certain qualities are especially important in a dog owner, and I have often thought about which are the most important. For a dog's well-being, how you interact is very important; that is, how you behave in the dog's eyes. I have always believed that loving a dog was the most important thing, but now I know that there is more.

LEADERSHIP

Today's popular TV programmes often emphasize the importance of our role as a "leader" and say that we should be "distinct". What this really means is that we should be harsh and hard, but this fact is camouflaged by words like "leader" and "distinct", which sound so much nicer. You may even hear cryptic words of advice such as "You have the responsibility – you cannot leave it to the dog." This is also just a paraphrase for "be firm and controlling". Unfortunately, such TV programmes make it sound as though this is the biggest and most important factor in a dog's life.

Nowadays, many talk about the importance of being a "leader". The fact is, we already are the dog's leader, because we have the same role and function as a leader in a wild canine group. Leaders in such a group are normally the parents. Now we are the "initiators", which means that we choose what activities the dog should engage in and when and where these should start and finish. For example, we decide when it is time to take a dog for a walk, where to go and when to return home. These, and a number of other things, are the reasons why the dog sees us as a "parent" and consequently a "leader". This means that the dog will never really "grow up" and continues to feel like a puppy in our family.

To be harsh, punishing and overpowering has nothing to do with leadership. It is just a sort of bullying, which not only makes the dog feel uncomfortable, but also damages your relationship with the dog.

KNOWLEDGE ABOUT DOG CARE AND DOG BEHAVIOUR

It is important to know how to meet a dog's physical needs, such as the right food and health care, how often it should go for walks and how much mental stimulation it needs. Nail cutting, tooth care, grooming and visits to the vet when you suspect that something is wrong are equally important.

You also need to know how dogs function, what needs they have, why they do what they do in various situations, and you must be aware of dogs' natural behaviours. This knowledge is crucial in the handling of a dog, so that we can help it adapt to its family and be happy.

Unfortunately, many dogs still have to live their lives with great limitations on their natural needs. Many dogs are left alone all day and do not get enough physical and mental stimulation. They suffer both physical and psychological abuse because of their owners, who lack knowledge of what a dog really needs.

It is easy to love a cute puppy, but you should not forget that this love must last its entire life. (Photo: Maurer)

LOVE

For a long time, I used to believe that the most important thing for a dog owner was to have a good heart combined with genuine love for their dog. When the love is there, the dog becomes an important member of the family and you consequently treat it with kindness and patience. You take your dog for long walks, and you stop and allow it to sniff at every "interesting odour spot". In short, you care for the dog, try to understand it and want to learn about all its needs and behaviours.

On occasion, I was present when an adult dog was introduced to a person who wanted to adopt it. At those times, I always gave priority to how "big a heart" the prospective dog owner seemed to have. Often, we first let another dog into the room. If the presumptive new owners stopped talking to people around and instead focused on greeting the strange dog, talking softly and tenderly to it, then I knew that they would give any dog a good home. Sometimes we let a slightly mischievous dog run into the room and jump up and greet the visitors. If they accepted the dog's wild rampage and laughed when it jumped up at them, we felt that they had passed the test.

However, I have begun to re-evaluate my general views on the qualities of a dog owner. Of course, I still think that love is important but, unfortunately, I have seen that this does not always stay constant throughout a dog's life. For many people the love seems to subside and burn out like a campfire running out of wood. Some people seem to change over time and begin to feel that their dog is something of a nuisance. As love decreases, irritation increases. So loving a dog when it is a cute puppy, or when it is convenient, as opposed to during its entire life are different things.

EMPATHY

Some people love their dogs when they are together with them, but when they are away doing other things, they seem to have forgotten all about them. This may cause even an extremely loving person to leave a dog at home alone all day. The dog might be heartbroken in its solitude, and bark and whine for the whole time. If people lack empathy, they forget about their dog when they do not see it. This is a classical case of "out of sight, out of mind".

Therefore, I believe that the ability to empathize with the dog's situation, and to understand how it feels even when you are not there, is just as important as the capacity for love. You should consider your dog's thoughts and feelings in every situation, even when you are not physically with him.

Body contact — quality contact

During one period of time, I helped a neighbour take her dogs out for walks. Afterwards, back at the house, I spread some treats on the yard for the dogs to find while I sat on the stairs and watched them. It surprised me, every time, how one of the dogs, who really loved food (to put it mildly), just searched briefly for the treats. She would rather come to me and sit or lie in my lap, just as she did when she was a little puppy. To be patted and caressed and feel closeness, warmth and have body contact meant so much more to her than anything else, even the tasty treats, which is a perfect example of how important body contact is.

FULFILMENT OF A BASIC NEED

Body contact is one of a dog's basic needs, and therefore is something that is essential for a dog and must be satisfied. This need becomes stronger the less the individual receives, as for example with food – the less you get the hungrier you will be.

Natural unfulfilled needs in young puppies do not seem to loosen their grip on the individual as they get older, but become a priority and never seem to be quite fulfilled. What was missing or not sufficient during infancy cannot be fully replaced later on in life. It continues to be a strong need in the future. This is well known in human psychology, but you also see it in other animals.

In one experiment, half a group of puppies got milk from baby bottles with large holes – they did not have to make much of an effort to suck them. Those in the other group had to work harder to get milk, because they had bottles with small holes in the rubber tip. The puppies who drank their milk quickly and easily, without much suckling, continued to want to suck on different things even into adulthood. The conclusion was that the suckling need must be satisfied, otherwise it will continue.

Dog psychologist David Selin investigated whether or not a dog's howling was a natural need. He had noticed that dogs howl when a security alarm starts to sound. He tested whether a dog was willing to work in order to trigger the alarm. With the help of an intricate track, the dog had to climb up rickety crates in order to reach a lever with which the alarm could be triggered. Using this method, Selin could see whether the dog had a wish to trigger the alarm in order to start howling at it. It turned out that the dog worked hard to get this instinctive need satisfied.

HARLOW'S EXPERIMENT

American psychologist and behavioural researcher Harry Harlow did an experiment with Rhesus monkeys in the late 1950s in which he demonstrated the importance of body contact (16).

The experiment's objective was to find out about how we measure love, or attachment to our parents. Harlow studied infant monkeys who had no contact with their real mothers, but instead were provided with surrogate mothers – one made of cotton which just provided comfort and another, a "wire doll", which just provided food. The baby monkeys were given milk from bottles that were stuck on the wire mother. In the experiments, the baby monkeys preferred the cloth mothers to food that was necessary for life. The experiment showed that comfort plays a very

Body contact is a basic need and especially important for puppies. (Photo: Shutterstock)

important role in an infant's life. All psychological, social and sexual functions were adversely affected by not having close contact with a real mother.

Later research has confirmed these results and partly also shown how this close contact works. It represents an important feeling of security and safety, it has a calming, stress-reducing effect on the nervous system, and it also strengthens the psychological bonds among individuals in a group. The need for close body contact, love and affection is just as important for dogs as it is for people.

A FEELING OF SECURITY

To have an adult nearby means protection and safety for an infant. It is to the grown-up that the child or baby animal runs when danger threatens. Most mothers in the animal kingdom have special warning sounds to tell their babies to either "freeze or hide", or to come back to them as fast as they possibly can.

Body contact and touch against soft fur or skin is an impulse that communicates this extremely important feeling of security. This is a conclusion made by researchers that have investigated what pets mean to human beings (1).

One aspect of the positive experience of close contact is the effect of the release of endorphins, morphine-like substances produced by the body which, among other things, have a calming effect. Even the neurotransmitter oxytocin makes you experience pleasant feelings; its level

increases in individuals in close body contact, as well as with massage and caresses. This happens with everybody, young and old, and of course with mother and child during breastfeeding.

When a person pets a dog, not only does the pulse lower in the person doing the petting, but also in the dog. A recent study in a dog pound in Dayton, Ohio, USA showed that body contact and petting prevented an increase of the stress hormone cortisol. People who give massage to

Quality time for your dog

It is important to give dogs plenty of time for close contact, especially when they are puppies, but you must not forget that older dogs have this need too. When you sit down with your dog and stroke its fur, massage it, let it lie in your lap and pay attention to it, it is quality time spent together.
If you own several dogs there is a risk that you will not have enough time for this important part of your social relationship, in which case you have to make a bigger effort or engage other family members or friends in actively socializing with your dogs.

Having a dog improves the prognosis of heart patients. The most important factor in this regard is body contact. (Photo: Shutterstock)

dogs emphasize that it often has a calming effect and increases the psychological contact with the animals.

HEART PATIENTS WITH DOGS

The chances of surviving a heart attack increase if you own a dog or a cat, and American scientists gave credit to body contact as being the most important factor (10). To have someone to caress, feel warmth and affection from and to give back to is crucial. For human beings body contact is

sometimes seen as taboo, governed by unwritten rules in society, if not within the family – and even here, it is not always good. However, the need is there and it will not disappear; on the contrary, it increases when it is never satisfied. Close contact with animals is not limited by any social rules and can take place without restrictions anywhere and at any time.

IMPORTANT FOR THE YOUNG

Body contact is especially important for infants, regardless of species, and provides physical protection against danger. Baby animals and children cannot defend themselves. They are completely dependent on their parents, primarily their mother.

Nearly all children seek body contact with animals, which proves that they wish to fulfil a need. It is also common for young children to have a cuddly toy they want to be close to and get comfort from, especially if they feel lonely. An important component of a cuddly toy is its soft fur. A wire doll would work just as poorly for a child as it did for the monkeys in Harlow's experiment.

Mirror of the soul

"Mirror neurons" are tiny brain cells; without them, we would not be able to feel empathy or be compassionate. These mirror neurons are possibly the most delicate essence of the soul and the crowning result of millions of years of evolution. Some neuroscientists say that perhaps these brain cells are what separate us from other animals; that only human beings can understand and feel empathy for another individual (19).

WE ARE NOT AS UNIQUE AS WE THINK

It is often said that humankind is the crown of creation and that we are the highest form of species on earth, although this might be hard to argue when you look at the world and all the cruelty and violence created by humans. But even though we can be considerate, understanding and respectful towards other people, sadly, not all people feel the same about animals. The belief in the old days was that animals could not experience much pain, sorrow and suffering. Now we know better.

Recent research has found that humans are not the only species with mirror neurons in their brains. Dogs, among other species, have them too! This means that dogs have a certain ability to feel empathy, to care and act altruistically without expecting any personal award. When you dig deeper and learn more about dogs you will find that they have precisely these abilities. They prove it constantly with their actions.

I have seen it countless times, for instance with the female Border Collie Lajban. I helped train her to be the first service dog in Sweden. During the years, she worked out, all by herself, how to push her owner's wheelchair. She figured out that she could move the chair forward when she placed her neck against the back of the chair and pushed hard. (Although her owner did help to move the chair forward.) Lajban stopped now and then when she was pushing the chair and looked ahead, as if she was checking to see whether there were any obstacles ahead.

Control instead of unpredictability

To be able to foresee what is going to happen is just as important for dogs as for human beings. If you have scheduled walks, feeding times and activities this has a stress-reducing effect.

In a series of experiments, animals were exposed to uncomfortable situations such as electric shocks (38). If these happened at the same time every day, and were preceded by a warning, such as the sound of a tone, the negative effects of these stressful events were not so severe. As long as the animals knew what was going to happen they seemed to be mentally prepared to deal with it.

If the animals in these experiments were not able to foresee the uncomfortable situation ahead, because it happened randomly and without any warning, it quickly led to such serious stress that the animals died of heart failure, ulcers or other stress-related diseases.

The same destructive results were achieved when the researchers let the animals hear the warning sound, but did not follow up with the electric shock. It was equally stressful when what the animals expected to happen never happened.

Dogs show an increased level of the negative stress hormone cortisol when they are exposed to unpredictable unpleasant events (23).

The essential feeling of being in control over your life situation is also an important factor in reducing negative stress. Even if animals are exposed to unpleasant events, they avoid serious stress if they are able to be in control of the situation.

Experiments show that if they can avoid electric shocks by escaping to a "safe" corner of the cage or by pushing a button, they will not suffer serious symptoms.

DAILY ROUTINES ARE IMPORTANT

Most families have daily routines for their dog. Mealtimes and walks usually happen around the same time, and they are always preceded by the same signals. There will be a clatter with the food bowls and words like "Come and get your food",

Daily routines, for example always feeding at the same time, reduce stress. (Photo: Shutterstock)

Deciding for itself where and how long it sniffs interesting spots gives the dog a sense of being in control. (Photo: Shutterstock)

and fetching the leash, getting your coat and saying something like "Let's go for a walk".

It is interesting to add more routines if you can. Always resting after a meal is a routine that dogs quickly learn and seem to appreciate. Whether it's a short or long rest doesn't matter. To activate a dog mentally indoors a couple of times a day at the same time is also a good routine which the dog looks forward to. For instance, you can place small treats in boxes or bags, or have your dog search for treats in one or several rooms.

LET THE DOG FEEL IN CONTROL

If your dog feels in control over its life then you have managed to "vaccinate" it against negative stress and added a little extra joy, security and self-esteem.

When you take a walk, allow your dog to stop and sniff as often and as long as it wants. Let the dog decide the direction of the walk

A bit of change is nice

Occasionally, it is a good idea to let your dog experience other things in addition to its everyday activity, such as a trip in the car, visiting others or having guests at your house. These breaks in its daily routine usually happen during the weekend, when life changes for everyone in the family.

whenever possible. Then it will also have a sense of being in control – after all, it is the dog's walk, not yours! Focus on your dog – not your mobile – during these special moments together.

Be observant of small signals when your dog is trying to express that it is hungry, it wants to go outside for a walk, wants to play, wants to sit next to you on the couch, etc. Unfortunately, most people miss these signals and consequently a dog stops communicating.

Rank order and leadership

We are accustomed to thinking "vertically" in terms of relationships among dogs. This means that we assume that there is a "pecking order" from the high to lower ranking animals, and that this power or rank order always goes from the top down, like steps on a ladder.

However, time has passed and we know more today. Ethologists agree that rank order is "horizontal" and to a greater degree based on age. The hierarchical order is in fact reversed – in other words, it is not the dominant behaviour of "higher ranking individuals" that decides who is the boss. On the contrary, it is the younger and "lower" individuals that with their active submissive behaviour show that they are "lower".

The biologist Thelma Rowell was the first to point out that it is not a question of "dominance order" in a wild pack of animals, but rather a question of "submission order" (31). Ethologists often emphasize that this rank order concept as a model does not fully explain the relationships within a wolf pack (25).

WORDS THAT MISLEAD US

Words such as "dominance" and "submission" are established ethological terms. They mean that an individual has or does not have access to a resource, for example food or a sexual partner. This resource is usually accessible without using threats or violence, but by using social competence, cleverness, experience and age.

Dogs can be clever and can figure out a way to gain access to certain resources. I have witnessed this myself a couple of times. On one occasion one of a family's dogs was chewing happily on a nice new bone from the butcher's. The other dog had also been given a bone, but it was not as big as his friend's bone. He looked enviously at the other dog and started circling around him. It was as if he was trying to figure out a way to steal the bone. Suddenly he dashed off barking like crazy at something in the distance. But there was nothing there. The dog with the big bone stopped chewing, looked up and ran in the same direction, also barking. The clever dog circled back and snatched the bigger bone, very pleased with himself.

Dominance:

To many people the word "dominance" equates to "suppression", threats or biting. However, that is a misinterpretation. Dominant animals are less aggressive than animals of lower status. The parental couple in a wolf pack have the highest status, which means that they are the most dominant, and they show the least aggression of the entire pack.

Submission:

The ethological term "submission" is not synonymous with fear or with giving in to someone stronger or of a higher status. It is a generic term for a series of body signals and sounds that illustrate a temporary position in relation to another individual.

It can either involve "passive submission" – meaning that you show a "peace flag" and are not intending to compete for a resource. It can also be "active submission" – where you "court" another individual. Adult dogs use submissive signals similar to those of puppies. They use tail wagging and licking of the mouth of the other dog, low body posture, the ears and the corner of the mouth pulled back, and yelping sounds. It looks like an expression of love and joy, and it may mean just that. In these signals also lies an enforcement of the psychosocial bonds that exist between these individuals. A perfect time to see this is when you come home and your dog greets you with "active submission".

There is no hidden judgement in these behaviours; nothing is "cowardly" or negative, and the dog is not "defeated". That would be to ascribe human attributes to dogs. Dogs do not lose face, only people feel they do that!

Leadership:

Are you among those who think that leadership is important? If so, it is time to rethink this, because it is just a myth. To say that "poor leadership" is behind problem behaviour is an unscientific diagnosis, and let us hope that it soon disappears.

To be the leader of your dog has, from an ethological point, nothing to do with power. And it has nothing to do with punishing and controlling the dog.

OUTDATED RESEARCH

Studies carried out from the 1920s onwards are the basis for our perception that rank order among social animals is based on power. These studies emphasized that animals of a higher rank are those that make most decisions and get the most food and other advantages. They claimed that the research showed that the strongest individuals set the law.

However, not all biologists were of the same opinion. Of course, many had seen signs of aggression in groups of animals in various studies. Moreover, they also saw that the strongest, most aggressive and cleverest individuals seemed to have most power in the group. However, they had also noticed the opposite! They saw that animals of high status were not aggressive and were not forceful. How could animals of the same species behave so radically different?

It was the biologist Thelma Rowell who pointed out why research studies could give such different results (31). The studies showing that an animal's rank order depended on aggression had been carried out on animals in captivity!

Studies on canines living in the wild showed completely different results. The biologist Adolph Murie had for instance, in the 1940s, emphasized that the individuals in the wolf pack he had studied showed hardly any aggression towards each other. On the contrary, he pointed out that he was surprised by the group's seemingly loving and close relationships (28).

THE DIFFERENCE BETWEEN FREEDOM AND CAPTIVITY

A group of animals in the wild, for instance a pack of wolves, is a family unit. It consists of mother, father and offspring of various ages that have survived, stayed or returned to the family after a period of roaming. In a few packs, non-family wolves had been "adopted".

The pack's ability to maintain peace and friendship is crucial for their survival, and every conflict threatens to weaken the group. Therefore, fights between wolves in a family are very rare.

Animals in zoos have not chosen the other members of their group, and they are often unrelated to each other. It is unnatural when there are too many individuals of the same age in a wolf pack. In addition, they cannot choose to leave, so they are forced to stay in a group with perhaps bad social relations. These wolves seldom or never get a chance to hunt, so they are constantly under-stimulated. Furthermore, they are not dependent on each other for survival. This is why there are fights and rejection processes in groups of wolves in captivity.

OLD MYTHS ABOUT RANK ORDER AND LEADERSHIP

The misconception that we, as dog owners, are part of a rank order and need to be on top of this hierarchy comes from older studies. And this has led to a number of weird myths, all of which have no basis in reality.

- Because human beings normally strive for higher status, at least at work, we have "humanized" our dogs and given them the same attribute.
- The conclusion was that if you were too kind to your dog it would advance in the rank order scale. WRONG!

· This way of thinking also led people to believe that if a dog is disobedient it is challenging your leadership. WRONG!
· A disobedient dog should then not only be corrected, but also punished hard, because that is the way you show them that you are the leader. WRONG!

People with a tougher and less empathetic outlook on dogs have naturally bought into this concept completely – it fits them like a glove.

· They are authoritarian with their dogs, but they justify it by equating it with "being a good leader".
· They often punish their dogs, but justify this as "showing leadership".
· They do not allow their dogs much freedom and would rather they were passive (not seen or heard too much). And they justify this as "correct leadership".
· They believe that the diagnosis "problem dog" is a sign of "bad leadership" and consequently they think that the best therapy is to practise better leadership, which for them means being tough and punishing the dog.

Nearly all TV programmes on dog behaviour today are focused on the importance of being a leader, and you hear phrases such as "Are you the leader of the pack?" No wonder that viewers believe that the most important thing is leadership. If it is on television it cannot be wrong ... can it?

MODERN ETHOLOGY

Biologists, ethologists, psychologists and many others educated in the field of animal behaviour have for many years tried to point out that the leadership theory is false. Nevertheless, so far we have had a hard time getting the message across. The fact is that despite all current scientific proof to the contrary, there are still people who write books and submit articles to dog magazines who stick to the misconception that "leadership" is essential.

The model that dogs seem to benefit most from is of course the "natural model" found in groups of animals living free in the wild. This also gives them space for personal development. The natural model is based on love and unity. This means that dog owners should not take out their bad temper on a dog. Do not let any feelings of prestige into the relationship with your dog. Do not think that the dog "wins" if it growls or if it wins the toy after a game of tug-of-war.

Canines are not programmed for the "prison model", even if they live in some sort of imprisonment with us. Nevertheless, they seem to cope with it.

BE A TEACHER – NOT A LEADER

Normal fostering and training has nothing to do with us being a leader and the dog a subordinate. It is simply a question of us being teachers and helping the dog to gain certain abilities. Something as simple as training a dog to refrain from doing something can be done in a positive way, without raising the voice or showing anger.

BE A PARENT – NOT A LEADER

Among wild canines, for instance wolves, the older animals in the pack do not take on much of a teacher's role. They are primarily parents and, as such, they demonstrate by their own behaviour how to behave. They are role models – and they are tolerant! In a wolf pack, all individuals mature in a natural way. When the young reach sexual maturity, they are adults, even if they lack the experience that comes with time. At this point, most of them leave their families and wander around to find a partner and establish a territory of their own.

Our domestic dogs do not develop like this. They do not become "adults" like wolves. They remain in their puppy relationship with us, which means that they treat us the same way as all puppies do

It is perfectly fine if the dog wins a game of tug-of-war. This will not change its feeling of respect towards its owner. (Photo: Maurer)

From the dog's point of view, the owner is definitely the "leader". (Photo: Shutterstock)

when socializing with those older than themselves. The reason for this is uncertain, but perhaps some of it is due to domestication. We have conditioned the dog to adapt to our way of living and bred them so that their mannerisms remain "puppy-like". Another reason could be that dogs do not leave us when they reach sexual maturity. They stay with us in the family and we will always be older, and therefore apparently wiser, than they are – at least if we look at it from their point of view.

YOU CAN RELAX!

What has been said in the sections above means you do not have to worry about the dog "taking charge", and you do not have to be "strong and show that you are the boss".

During training, you can fill your pockets with treats – if you like. And you can be as kind and loving as you want. In fact, it is totally okay to spoil your dog, within limits of course!

Yes, you are in fact already the dog's "leader", or whatever we may choose to

The leader's role and special tasks and activities in wild canines	Corresponding activities for a dog owner	Important activities for a dog owner to schedule
Initiates movement	Initiates a walk outside and other activities	Take the initiative to go on walks
Leads the group to hunting grounds etc.	Takes walks with a certain goal, leading to interesting activities	Go to places that stimulate mental activation, via goals or "stations". Use quick activities mixed with more focused ones, for instance agility, nose work, balancing, problem-solving and learning
Picks the prey	Chooses suitable activities (mental activation)	Choose different activities each day – sometimes quick, sometimes slow
Starts the hunt	Gives the "go ahead" signal to the dog	Let the dog wait shortly before the "okay" signal. Give a massage before
Cooperates during the hunt	Takes part in the activities with the dog	Follow the dog during activities. Direct it during agility exercises (with real or natural obstacles) or while searching, for instance for a dummy. Variation is best
Finishes the hunt	Ends the activities	If needed, finish activities with some stretching
Seldom starts social interactions, but does not reject those that occur	Lets the dog greet him/her and responds, but seldom initiates the greeting	Always make sure you let your dog greet family members and take other initiatives for social behaviour and normal rituals for dogs
Often subjected to attention and admiration	Reacts positively when the dog seeks contact	Be attentive to the dog's behaviour. When it is trying to seek attention, for instance with a glance, or by touch with a paw or its nose, be sure to respond, ask the dog to "show" you what it wants
Finds places to sleep, and inspires the rest of the group to rest (coordination)	Rests at certain times and encourages the dog also to relax	Relax together
Feeds the young	Feeds the dog	Feed the dog (at least twice a day)

call it. The reason is that you, from the dog's point of view, are older and have better social competence. Even if the dog came to you as an adult, it will see you as older and therefore wiser.

In addition to your role as a "parent" you are the instigator, in most situations, of the jobs and activities typical of a parent couple in a wolf family, as illustrated in the list below.

Gender roles of wolves

As cousins to our dogs, wolves are always interesting. That does not mean that the two species are alike. On the contrary, there are big differences between dogs and wolves. However, what these canines do have in common is fascinating – the wild and the domesticated species are of the same origin.

Apart from the similarities and dissimilarities, it is something intriguing and enticing to learn more about the ancestors of our dogs – it is like looking more closely at the stem of a beautiful flower.

THE MALE USED TO BE GLORIFIED

Not too long ago many still thought that a female wolf's most important role was to take care of her young, otherwise she was not really that important in the life of a wolf pack.The male, on the other hand, was believed to be essential to the survival of the whole pack. The general opinion was that he initiated any activity and led

the group in the hunt. It was also assumed that he was a firm teacher, that he protected his family with his courage, his power and his strength. Such were the beliefs at a time when most biologists, instructors and dog trainers were men.

However, in those days many of the studies were done on wolves in captivity. Now we know that wild animals and those in captivity cannot be compared in terms of behaviour and social interactions.

ETHOLOGICAL RESEARCH IS MAKING PROGRESS

Knowledge about wild wolves is constantly growing, thanks to new interesting observations. For instance wolves were reintroduced to Yellowstone National Park in the US states of Wyoming, Montana and Idaho during the 1990s, initially in 1995 (9). Their progress and impact on the park's ecosystem have been followed ever since.

The existence of the wolves has had only positive effects on both nature and wildlife. References are made to the "cascade effect", that is, how one species affects another and then how this affects a third, and so on.

The reintroduction of wolves to Yellowstone helped restore the ecological balance. The number of elks decreased, the surrounding natural environment grew healthier, insects and birds increased in numbers. Scientists have been able to ascertain that wolves and other predators are important and necessary. Native

Wolves are loving parents. (Photo: Shutterstock)

Americans in Canada and Alaska have a saying: "The wolf keeps the caribou (reindeer) healthy".

Wolf packs are very skilled hunters. These family-oriented animals keep together and cooperate efficiently. The young are protected and cared for in the best possible way. They are not "fostered" and brought up by demanding, harsh parents that dominate their offspring. The parents are monogamous, and if one of them dies it is unlikely that the survivor will find a new mate.

In a wolf pack, everybody takes part in everything. They all hunt, carry home food to the waiting cubs, and mother or nurse the young. They all share in taking care of the cubs; they all warn and protect the group. Yet researchers have found that wolves have a way of dividing tasks among them. Previously, it was thought (and some people still do think) that the male is the most important member of the pack. Now we know that the female's role is more important (9). There is a splendid cooperation and "democracy" among all members of the pack, which probably explains why they are such successful animals.

Studies also confirm that the parent couple do not force the others to follow them. In his book "The Wolf" (published in 1970), wolf researcher David Mech talks about a pack preparing to cross an ice-covered lake (26). The parent couple walked out on the ice, but the younger animals hesitated and remained on the beach. After having tried a couple of times to encourage them to follow, the parents finally gave up and followed where their young ones wanted to go.

NEW VIEWS ON GENDER ROLES

In most packs, the father, normally the oldest male, will lead the group to various hunting grounds. He does not always run at the front of the pack. Many of the younger animals who are full of energy also take the lead, although the parents know where they are going, in this case to the best hunting ground. Nevertheless, the father is often the first to defend the others if a large predator, such as a bear or a mountain lion, threatens them.

The vast majority and weight of responsibility falls on the female. Observations in Yellowstone National Park have shown that in general it is the female that sets up a new territory after she has left her own family around the age of one and a half years (9). Then she waits for a suitable roaming male. Not all wolves that meet end up as a couple; it seems that some love in the air is also required.

Within her chosen territory, the female also finds the best place to deliver her cubs. She often digs out a den in a sand bank, but it could also be a very simple den under the roots of a fallen tree. This is a crucial and important role. She has to choose a place where the cubs are safe from other predators. It must not be near a bear's den, below an eagle's nest or where a mountain lion lives. The den must be somewhere where there is no risk of rain or melted ice water drowning the cubs. It also has to be secure enough to stop large predators from entering.

The responsibility for the survival of the cubs during their first weeks lies with the mother. She has to be healthy and give them the care they need to survive and grow. If she should die, there is, however, a chance that another adult female could take over her role. This is possible thanks to a phenomenon called "false pregnancy", in which mature females act as though they are pregnant and start producing the hormone progesterone. Finally, they also produce milk. Perhaps this is nature's way of securing the survival of the cubs.

The female also seems to take most of the initiative during the hunt, such as choosing the prey and starting the attack. Their team play is incredibly sophisticated, with lots of eye contact and changing of tactics depending on the behaviour of their prey.

So, that is the current view on the gender roles among wolves, in which the female clearly seems to be the most important and take the most initiative. However, this can differ between packs, and gender roles can have variations within a wild-living pack. Knowledge is perishable and there are always new things to learn.

Your role as a role model

We have talked about our role as a dog owner, leader and parent. Most of us try to live up to these roles, and be a good dog owner, a good leader and a good parent.

As mentioned, in recent years the leadership role has been over-emphasized, but it now seems that our role as "parents" of the

Puppies learn a lot by mimicking their mother's behaviour. (Photo: Shutterstock)

dog is getting more attention. However, the importance of another role becomes more apparent as more research is available, and that is the one of being a role model.

MOTHER'S INFLUENCE

We have known for a long time that puppies take after their mothers. Their father is often not there, but if he was there from the start they would take after him as well, or after another "father figure". It is estimated that puppies learn about 30 percent of what they know from their mother, so she has a considerable influence.

We also know that dogs have the ability to mimic each other's behaviour. For instance, when sheep farmers want to train a young dog, they use an older, well-trained herding dog to show the younger ones how to work with sheep. Many hunters do the same thing when they want to train young hunting dogs.

LEARNING BY EXAMPLE

The common belief in earlier times was that adult dogs could not learn by just watching other dogs, only puppies could do that. But the Hungarian ethologist Adam Miklósi was able to prove that a dog can study what another dog or a person does and then repeat that behaviour (27). For instance, one dog watched as another dog worked out how to get a treat out of a closed box. By watching, the second dog learned how to solve the same problem faster.

Wolves are not considered to be as good at learning detailed tasks as dogs are. This ability seems to be unique to dogs, perhaps because of thousands of years of domestication. However, we do know that the parental animals in a wolf pack teach their young by just being role models, not only in terms of how to hunt and survive but also how to function socially.

In conclusion, and as pointed out earlier, those who insist that wolf mothers raise their young using dominant behaviour including growling and biting are wrong. Human beings are the only animals that use authority when raising their offspring.

LIKE MOTHER, LIKE DAUGHTER

Dogs that have not been well taken care of by their own mothers end up not being such good mothers themselves. If a female dog is sick and therefore irritated and short-tempered with her puppies, they might become emotionally disturbed. They, in turn may be short-tempered with their own puppies (24).

The same thing most probably often happens in families where the dog owners are authoritarian, demanding, hard and domineering towards their female dogs by using punishment and a harsh demeanour. There is a risk that these female dogs will treat their puppies in the way they were treated by their owners.

Dog mothers are kind to a fault. Think about it. How would it look if they domi-

nated, restricted, growled and controlled their puppies? The consequence would be that their puppies became passive and scared of being punished for doing something wrong. They would grow up with low self-confidence. If they were living in the wild, they would for instance not be good at hunting. They would not dare to attack large prey, and they would function so poorly that their weakened chances of survival would threaten the whole group.

PERFECT ROLE MODELS

Wolf parents are role models and their puppies take after them. Since the social interaction in the family is friendly and harmonious, the puppies learn to be friendly, cooperative and to avoid conflict. They learn social competence by taking after their parents and older siblings. Younger members of the pack of course learn to hunt from the older ones.

How you interact and socialize with your dog is of utmost importance when it is a puppy. However, new findings prove that, even after the puppy stage, this seems to be of greater importance than was earlier believed. The dog mimics how you function socially. If you are friendly, you will have a friendly dog.

Many dog experts think that the dog becomes problematic if you are not firm enough and you don't "put it in its place". This is wrong! You can and certainly should treat your dog with kindness. This

We are role models for our dogs; therefore, we need to treat them with kindness if we want them to be friendly. (Photo: Shutterstock)

It has been scientifically proven that positive methods, including clicker training, are very efficient in dog training. (Photo: Maurer)

tect everything that belongs to it. On the other hand, if you make no fuss about it, the puppy learns kindness and that it is not necessary to protect things.

You are a role model from day one. Be aware of this, and you will end up having a dog with good social competence.

The softies win!

There seems to be a constant war between those who advocate modern methods, representing positive training, on the one side, and the more conservative people on the other. The latter group claim that the old, harsher, methods, often shown on TV, are the best. Today, however, there is a lot of scientific evidence that supports the modern, softer methods. And this comes from ethology, psychology and medicine.

Those who propagate the more rigid methods do not call themselves hard; they want to be considered as being "natural" in their approach. They behave towards dogs as they believe that canines in the wild behave towards one another. A common argument is that you must be firm with your dogs, because dog mothers are supposedly firm with their puppies.

In fact, there is a depth of strong evidence to show that the proponents of the soft method are right: strong in the sense that the evidence is based on facts derived from modern research and deep in the sensethat these facts can be found in several disciplines, such as ethology, psychology and medicine.

does not make it aggressive, but friendly. Aggression does not come because you are kind. It builds up if you are too demanding and correcting. There are proven connections between authoritative fostering and behavioural problems – both with dogs and with children (5).

When a puppy growls and shows its teeth because you are too close to the food bowl or a bone, you should refrain from responding with anger. If you respond with anger, the dog will learn to be aggressive and pro-

ETHOLOGY

If we look at the dog mother, there is very little dominance in her behaviour towards her puppies. A study that argued that the dam could be rather tough with her puppies was based on litters kept in pens, where the bitch could not escape from her puppies (40). Other studies, on both wild canines and domestic dogs, show that the mother is very caring and patient with her young, at least until they are nine or ten weeks of age (13), and often even after that time. Ethologists have not been able to see dominance other than in excep-

tional cases, nor have they seen any attempts at fostering. Bitches that growl and even bite their puppies are generally sick and in pain. Despite their pain, these mothers are usually still not rough with their little ones.

The wolf is the dog's closest relative and there are many studies and observations on how they function socially. Adolph Muries findings in the 1940s, when he followed a pack of wild wolves, are still relevant (28). Wolf packs are a close-knit family unit with loving relationships and very little aggression. When fights occur, it is usually over lack of resources, for instance food or sexual partners.

Dogs like to cooperate with humans. There is no need to force them to do so. (Photo: Shutterstock)

Today, biologists and ethologists have been able to prove that the widespread opinion regarding the importance of rank order and leadership is wrong. There is no power hierarchy in the sense that the ones at "the top" rule over those with a lower "status". Instead, younger wolves show that they look up to their elders. They demonstrate this with a number of acts and body signals that we call "active submission". They are all expressions of joy and appreciation. Your dog goes through the same rituals when it welcomes you home with jumps and happy dances.

For the dog as a species, and as a relative of the wolf, unity is very important. Too much trouble and confrontation in a wolf pack would risk their chances of survival. Instead, they demonstrate various behaviours meant to strengthen the unity of the group, such as play, grooming and other body contact. Teeth are generally never used against anyone in the family, but there are some warning and threatening body language signals if trouble should arise. The instinctive bite inhibition we see with young animals is very strong.

However, there are incidents with dogs when bite inhibition has failed, resulting in severe damage to other dogs or people. These incidents can sometimes be explained by excessive inbreeding, primarily in popular breeds. In other cases, it has to do with sick dogs suffering from pain, or dogs living in a stressful and dysfunctional environment.

In other words, we need to acknowledge that the dog is peaceful, cooperative and adaptable. Authoritarian demands, punishment-based training and "leadership" do not correspond with the canine personality. On the contrary, your dog will be happy to learn and work together with you without using discipline, because that is its nature.

PSYCHOLOGY

That which many see as a "leadership problem" – in the sense of us being too yielding and indulgent with our dogs – is really a problem related to learning and training. If, for instance, a dog chases after a jogger in the park it has nothing to do with your "leadership". You just have not trained the particular behaviour that is desired in this situation. Therefore, what the dog did has nothing to do with whether or not you were firm; the dog just follows a natural hunting instinct to chase after something that moves fast.

A common misunderstanding is that you can get rid of a behaviour using punishment. Countless studies state this is not the case. Punishment may temporarily stop a certain behaviour, but it does not affect what the dog wants to do. It does not take long before the dog returns to the unwanted behaviour. A behaviour disappears with the help of systematic training based on positive reinforcement of an alternative behaviour. After that, the problem seldom returns.

Every time you punish the dog, it will result in an unexpected and unwanted effect. It damages your relationship and it can make the dog afraid of you. The dog may become submissive and afraid to take the initiative. It also dampens the dog's general ability to communicate. Above all, too much conflict, correction and punishment make the dog passive. An unfortunate effect drawing current research attention is that dogs that have been punished tend to develop more problem behaviours – which may include aggression against other dogs or people.

Research findings in psychology are consequently on the side of the "softies". Those who control, correct, punish and are authoritarian with dogs have no scientific proof on their side.

MEDICINE

Until now not many people have realized that authoritarian training may also result in medical problems for the dog. Many of these problems can last for a variable period. The use of a choke collar or slip lead, or even a normal collar, depending on how you handle the leash, can be dangerous and risk severe damage (30, 34). These injuries can be so serious that it is currently recommended that the leash is attached to a harness instead of a collar.

During unpleasant experiences, the amount of the stress hormone cortisol increases in the blood. Single negative experiences fade away, but with repeated oppressive, uncomfortable and scary events, the cortisol level is increased for much longer. It was noted in a Dutch study that the level of cortisol did not go down forseveral months after trainers stopped using an electric collar (32).

Dogs should be allowed to take the initiative, for example by drawing our attention to their food bowl. (Photo: Shutterstock)

Cortisol influences the digestive system and the heart. Even the immune system is affected. This means that dogs with a high cortisol level in their blood have an increased risk of becoming ill.

Those in favour of "hard" training methods often do not exercise their dogs as much as people in favour of "soft" training methods. Their dogs are often kept in dog runs, where they have no stimulation and cannot move around very much. Exercise, however keep dogs healthy; too little increases the risk of disease.

OBEDIENCE AND TRAINING

Dogs often differ significantly in their behaviour depending on the level of disciplinary training they have had. As already mentioned, the more punishment, correction and control the dog is exposed to, the greater the risk that problem behaviours occur.

Unfortunately, effects that are even more negative may develop. If a dog is cor-rected repeatedly, it will stop taking the initiative and will become dependent

Dogs that snatch food from the table cannot be "cured" successfully by punishment. (Photo: Shutterstock)

on the owner in all of its activities. Such a dog is afraid of being scolded and told to behave and be quiet. Dogs that are happy take the initiative. They might for instance rattle their food bowl for more food, or bark a little to say that they want to play or go outside.

The overly controlled dog will develop a "handler dependency" which will be a problem for anyone trying to train the dog for any kind of work, or task, where it needs to be able to work independently.

It is well known that your thoughts and ability to take the initiative help expand the brain's capacity for intelligent activity. A dog trained in an authoritarian way will not get a chance to experience stimulation of any brain capacity. As the dog gets older, it will lose more and more brain functions. These dogs have a shorter lifespan than those that are allowed to be active and take the initiative.

An authoritarian approach results in a passive dog that does not dare take any initiative and is completely dependent on its owner for something to happen. This means that the dog will be resting and waiting for the owner to initiate anything. It is common that such a dog will be resting for around 22 hours per day. When something finally happens, the dog will have so much pent up energy that it will overreact. This in turn will annoy the owner, who will punish the dog even more. It is a sad and vicious cycle, and one the dog will never win.

TREATING PROBLEM BEHAVIOUR

As mentioned, many people believe that you can cure problem behaviour by punishing the dog. This is wrong! If there is, for instance, a tempting steak or sausage on the table, the motivation to snatch it cannot be lessened by punishment, other than temporarily.

Certain TV programmes suggest that you should correct bad behaviour with punishment. This is wrong! It cannot be fixed in a day or in an hour. These quick-fix methods may be good for ratings, but the dogs are just "cured" temporarily. In addition, you risk creating other problem behaviours with these harsh methods, including choke collars, hitting the dog and other forceful methods.

The reality is that you can accomplish permanent results without hurting, suppressing or scaring the dog. You do this by analysing the reasons behind the problem behaviour and then working to create a suitable training programme built on positive reinforcement.

Treat or no treat?

For some reason, the issue of using treats in dog training has become controversial. Some people are against using them, while others think they are great. Those who do not like the use of treats call it a bribe, while the proponents call it a reward. Others change back and forth, depending on the prevailing opinion at the time.

Opponents argue: "You should not bribe the dog to obey. It should obey because we say so! And that's it!" Those who advocate the use of treats in training say "Come on! Of course the dog should be rewarded for a job well done!"

Psychology agrees with the people who are in favour of using treats in dog training. For dogs that like treats, it is an efficient reward. Most dogs like treats, but many over-masculine males may be hard to motivate with food.

LEARNING AND PERFORMANCE

It is necessary to differentiate between learning and performance. During the learning phase, it is very important to teach the dog with the help of encouragement and rewards.

Rewarding – not bribing

It is not a case of "to spoil" or "to bribe", but one of "to pay the dog for its work", which means teaching the dog by rewarding each step of progress.
A motivated dog feels happy during training and will of course learn faster and better. Treats have a lot to do with this and it is sad that not all dogs have a chance to be trained this way.

At first, the dog does not know what we want it to do. Treats are a perfect tool here. They keep the dog focused and motivated and help it to learn happily, willingly and quickly.

When the dog has learnt the task, treats are no longer that important but you should reward good behaviour anyway. After all, who wants to work without being paid? However, you do not have to use a treat every time. Sometimes you can replace the treat with an encouraging tone of voice or give the dog the opportunity to play with a toy instead.

MOTIVATION IS IMPORTANT

It is important for the dog to be motivated in order to perform. It is often enough to praise the dog, but not everybody is able to sound sufficiently encouraging. Therefore, it is good to use a variety of tools to sustain motivation. Another encouragement is to pet the dog, but with most dogs this does not seem to have the same positive effect as treats and an encouraging voice.

Another way of keeping up the level of motivation is immediately to reward a correct behaviour with play, perhaps a hunting game, such as throwing a ball for the dog to chase. Alternatively you can start a game of tug-of-war with a rag or a rope. However, dogs easily get stressed and unfocused by such activities so it should only be done for a short period of time.

It should be noted, however, that playing games is not always a good idea during the early stages of learning, depending on what you are trying to teach the dog. Play increases the production of stress hormones, which in turn may block parts of the brain where learning takes place. If there are exercises demanding concentration, the dog may become unfocused and, as a result, its learning ability suffers.

DIVERTING ATTENTION

Perhaps one valid criticism of the use of treats is when they are used in situations where you want to stop the dog from reacting to something. I am referring to exercises used to teach the dog to refrain from a certain behaviour, for instance to stop it attacking other dogs. In this case, you would use a treat to divert the dog's attention from the other dog.

This is not learning, but diversion. The treats are not given as a reward for something the dog did well. You are just diverting the dog's attention. If you do this for a long period of time you might achieve some results, but it usually takes much longer than if you reward the dog for doing something right.

The most efficient way is to maintain your distance from the other dog and talk encouragingly to your dog while passing them. Reward your dog the very second you have passed the other dog. Those who say that this does not work have just not placed themselves far enough away. If increasing the distance does not help and the dog still wants to attack the other dog, then it is time to seek the help of a dog psychologist.

SMALL IS GOOD ENOUGH

A common mistake is to use pieces of treats that are too big. Many believe that

Hunting games with their favourite toy can be a great motivation for dogs. (Photo: Shutterstock)

the bigger the treat, the bigger the reward. But it is the other way around: the smaller the treat – the bigger the reward. The reason why the dog seems to get excited over small pieces of treat is only partly because it will dampen its hunger. The dog also has to focus a little more to get the treat.

We are talking about treats three or four millimetres in size. For big dogs, they should perhaps be a little larger.

Treats from the store seldom work that well. Either they are not tasty enough, they are too hard to chew or too big.

If your dog has a favourite treat you do not have to change it. Otherwise, I would recommend making your own treats. You can boil fresh beef liver in water until it is cooked through. Let it cool, and then cut it in small pieces. Roast them in the oven, at 100 degrees Celsius, for a few minutes until the surface has dried – not the inside. When the pieces have cooled off you can freeze them in plastic bags. Now you always have delicious treats that your dog is willing to trade for its pedigree certificate.

TRAINING IS IMPORTANT, BUT ...

Dogs should be able to interact well with people – both adults and children. They should also be able to interact well with dogs and other animals. And they should not bark and disturb others. Of course, we need to train our dogs so that they fit well within our complex society. But the flip side of the coin is that there are as well drawbacks to training. These have not received much attention until now, even though the effects on dogs are significant. Therefore, this chapter will deal with the negative sides of training.

Some people look at dog training as a simple thing. They do not believe in being lenient, and think that you must show, even at puppy-stage, that you are the boss. Sadly, harsh methods, punishment and shouting at a dog are not the exception, but the rule.

Others try to tread more carefully and positively by finding a balance between punishment and praise. But they still feel that the most important thing is to have full control over the dog in all situations.

Finally, there are those people who do not feel that their own "prestige" is in danger if the dog does not obey immediately. For instance if they say "Come here!" and the dog does not respond because it is

(Photo: Maurer)

busy with something interesting, they do not make a big fuss about it. They allow the dog to have some will of its own.

Pros and cons of dog training

Nobody has really looked closely behind the scenes at dog training. Criticism is usually directed at the dogs, and you may hear comments such as "Those dogs are difficult to train" or "That breed is just too independent". More often than not, criticism is also directed at the dog owners: "That person cannot handle dogs at all" or "She spoils her dog far too much". Even dog-training class instructors may be criticized: "He is way too hard" or "She cannot control the people in the class".

However, the training methods themselves are very seldom questioned. It seems that the way we train our dogs is not supposed to be challenged. Perhaps this is because it is so difficult to come up with alternative methods. Using a leash in training still seems to be necessary wherever you look. However, for many years now I have been able to demonstrate that you can train dogs easily without using a leash.

The advantages of dog training are obvious. If dogs were not trained to follow the rules of society, then the criticism of those owning a dog would be so massive that we would not be allowed to have dogs as pets. However, contrary to popular belief, dogs would not become more aggressive if they lacked training and "leadership", although they would certainly do whatever they pleased. No training at all would probably result in disobedient but very happy dogs.

There are disadvantages with dog training, whether you do it yourself, take classes or consult a personal dog trainer. The fact is that, when we increase control over the dog it loses some control over its own life. Another disadvantage with training is that the dog becomes more passive, which unfortunately is often the goal. Many just want a calm and obedient dog.

ABOUT CONTROL

One of the essential ingredients for mental and physical health is to have a feeling of control over your life situation. This is important for both people and animals.

Small children have very little to say about their life situation; their behaviour is governed by adults. Older children and teenagers strive to feel that they are in control in a world filled with demands and conflicts. This relates to most social environments: family, school, groups of friends, authorities and all other instances that temporarily or constantly limit an individual's behaviour. This is why it is so rewarding for children to grow up with pets. Then they have someone to care for and they also learn responsibility.

Most adults are in control and take control, this is part of our mission in life and we are normally prepared for it. We call it responsibility. Adults who lose their sense of being in control usually end up with mental problems, such as aggression, irritability, depression and anxiety disorders.

The likelihood of being in control of your own life lessens the older you get, and people may become more dependent on the help of others. Elderly people who accept everything and refrain from showing any will of their own are the easiest for caretakers to handle. Those who protest and demand more attention will often be discouraged. Perhaps this is the reason why apathy and depression are common amongst those in older age groups.

However, when you give people a feeling of being in control of their life, their quality of life also increases significantly. Alternative teaching methods used in schools, for instance the Montessori method, have made children active, motivated and more self-confident. Where employees are allowed more influence in the workplace, the company records a lower number of sick days. Where elderly people are allowed to take part in making the decisions regarding the routines in their old people's home their quality of life as well as their lifespan increases.

Dogs must be trained to follow the rules of society so that they can cope with our everyday life. (Photo: Shutterstock)

Dogs are particularly easy to control – unfortunately. The behavioural synchronization found with animals living in groups is especially apparent in dogs. They are by nature passive, and they coordinate their activities with the rest of their group. You often see the younger individuals in the group synchronizing with the older ones. When the older members rest, the younger ones also rest. When the older ones are active, the younger ones follow. This is what is known as "structured passiveness" in wild animals and it does not result in under-stimulation. However, for our domestic dogs it leads to an unnatural amount of hours of rest during the day. This explains why mature dogs can rest all day long if you do not activate them. This is also the reason why dogs appreciate every activity so much, which makes it so easy for us to control their activities. We initiate play, walks and everything else – we control everything.

Humans have a great need for control, and one instrument is to take dog-training classes. Modern training is mainly positive and based on reward, but the goal is still to increase control. Praising the dog all the time during the training is also a form of control. Then it is hard for the dog to take initiatives of its own, and it loses its ability to influence the situation.

TRAINING IS PACIFYING

Dog training today is unfortunately laid out in such a way that the ultimate goal, for both dog owners and instructors, is to sup-press the puppy's or young dog's energy. This is also emphasized in newspaper articles, in TV programmes and in books.

The goal of obedience training is in fact to make the dog passive. There are exercises aimed at interrupting unwanted behaviour, such as not to pull on the leash, not to jump on people, not to bark and not to play with other dogs in the group. Most exercises are on the "no" side. When you look closer at the exercises you can easily see that they all are about dampening and calming a dog down and making it passive.

The dog owner's goal is also an important factor. He or she usually wants a "calm dog" that obeys on command and behaves like a "good dog". Furthermore, they wish to achieve this with as little effort as possible, which means that the instructor is pressurized to get results as quickly as possible. This in turn encourages the use of harder methods and short cuts in training, so called "quickfixes".

It does not take a lot of traditional training to make a dog passive.

When a dog starts to do something it is often because it needs to act out all of its pent-up energy. Often it will jump around, bite, tease or do something it is not supposed to do which will get a response from you. These kinds of initiative are dampened by training. Unfortunately, with this comes a risk of the dog becoming obedient in the sense of being "passive".

This is especially common with life indoors. If the dog runs around so that all the carpets are torn up, it will often be told to calm down and "Go to your bed!" It does

If the dog does something on its own initiative, it may lead to problems. The dog may for instance suddenly feel like running to greet another dog, run across the street, chase animals in the park or bark at someone that looks "suspicious". Therefore, it is necessary to train the dog, but it is equally important to avoid making it passive.

BANS AND PUNISHMENTS

High-energy dogs in particular are exposed to many "corrections". This often becomes a battle of wills, which usually the owner wins, sometimes with the help of a trainer. However, the more you punish, the bigger the risk of behavioural problems. This is the conclusion of several studies (5, 18). In a pilot study, where I was supervising one of my students, we were able to show that the more authoritarian the dog owner, the bigger the risk of the dog becoming aggressive towards other dogs.

Punishment has nothing to do with learning. It does not affect what the dog wants and it will not take long before the problem behaviour returns. Therefore, this is not the right approach if you want to change the dog's behaviour permanently. If you do, then you have to use a different training strategy based on reward and encouragement.

LEARNED HELPLESSNESS

As mentioned earlier, the American scientist and psychologist Martin Seligman developed the theory of "learned helpless-

Young dogs in particular are full of energy, which unfortunately is often suppressed through training. (Photo: Shutterstock)

not take long before the dog is completely passive in the home. Many think this is "a nice dog".

Something called "passiveness training" was introduced a few years ago and it has become popular. This means that the dog is trained to rest when you do. However, in some instances, the dog's own choice to rest has been replaced with coercion. Because dogs are passive by nature we do not need special training to make them more passive.

ness" following his studies of dogs that were placed in situations where they had no choice or viable alternative. They were exposed to unpleasant electric shocks with no means of escape (14, 32).

After a short period of being exposed to this torture, the personality of the initially happy and alert dogs changed. They became listless, passive and often depressed. They developed eating disorders, were afraid of sounds and had problems socializing with other dogs. Their immune systems were impaired and they were often sick.

To be able to feel in control of your life and the situations you end up in is crucial for physical and mental well-being. Martin Seligman commented after these studies that it seemed easy for dogs to fall into learned helplessness (33).

Feeling in control – or feeling helpless?

Where would you place your dog on a scale from 1 to 10?
Every limitation and controlling action moves the dog further towards helplessness.
Authoritarian training, lots of punishment and high demands literally drive the dog towards helplessness!

The importance of taking the initiative

People with an authoritarian view of dog training often warn others against allowing their dogs to take any initiative. Behind this thinking is the old view of rank order, the unscientific fear that the dog is going to "advance socially", get power and "take over". This is wrong and completely irrelevant and has been rejected by modern ethology and psychology.

It really is the other way around! We should allow our dogs to take the initiative – even encourage them to do so, as long as it does not lead to any unwanted behaviour. When the dog learns that we see and listen to it, then its important feeling of self-control also increases. Such a dog will be happier, more active and social and have a stronger immune system. Finally, yet equally important, the dog will have a much closer contact with its owner.

LADY

I would like to tell you about a six-year old Spaniel, let us call her Lady. I looked after her every day until she died of an illness at the age of eleven. Her owners moved into the house next door. One day I was surprised to see that they had a dog. I was surprised because I had never heard the dog or even seen it go out for a walk. The couple next door were gone for more than twelve hours a day and left a back door open to a small, concrete backyard where the dog could do her business. They were not "animal people" and Lady was their first dog. They never took her out for walks, so she hardly had any muscles. Mentally she was apathetic. She did not greet, did not play and was completely introverted. She ate and slept, and that had been her journey through life for six years.

I offered to look after her during the day-time while they were at work. Her owners accepted with a shrug and did not seem to understand the dog's need for company and to go for walks.

"Come on! Let's play!" (Photo: Maurer)

In the evening, I hid some treats in my house, which she loved to search for every morning. This quickly became her big and joyful morning ritual. Her little short stub of a tail wagged the entire time she was searching.

Now I wanted to see if she could communicate with me, if she could take the initiative and tell me that she wanted something. When she arrived one morning she immediately started to search for treats, but she could not find any. I had not hidden any the previous night. After she had searched for several minutes, her disappointment was obvious. I studied her from the couch while I felt incredibly guilty, but I persisted.

After a while, she came up to me with a surprised look and tilted her head. I asked, "Do you want to search for treats?" and immediately stood up. Then I fetched the goodie bag and started to hide some treats – to her great joy.

For the first time in her life, this mentally starved dog had a tool for reaching out to others. After this day, whenever she wanted something, for instance to go out, play, search for treats, get food or water, she came up to me with that special look and tilted her head. Just the way she had learned to do when the treats were not where they were supposed to be.

"SHOW ME"

In order to teach your dog to take the initiative you have to pay attention to small signals. Perhaps your dog just looks at

you; perhaps it yelps or seems worried. It could be because it wants you to do something, for instance fill its water bowl, its food bowl or take it for a walk.

If you are attentive to these small signals and follow the dog, then it will show you. If you are not sure what it wants it might be that it just wants something to happen. It might be bored or just have a lot of built-up energy racing inside its body.

Dogs "point" by looking in a certain direction. Unfortunately, it is common that dogs look at you as though you could read minds. But you can teach the dog to show you more clearly, perhaps by pawing on something. It could be on the door to the cupboard where the treat is stored or where the toys to play with are kept. So, when the dog seems to want something, say, "Show me" and just follow it.

IF THE DOG ITSELF GETS TO CHOOSE

There are so many tempting and interesting things for a dog to do during a walk, most of all smelling scents left by other dogs. Dogs clearly show when they want to reach a scent they have picked up, and the only thing stopping them from getting closer to it is you. Of course, you should let the dog go there, unless it is too inappropriate or inconvenient. After all, it is the dog's walk, not yours!

When you arrive at a crossroads, you can let the dog choose the direction. It just makes the dog feel good to be able to take such initiatives and feel in control of the situation. When it is not suitable to let the dog choose, then give it a trat to follow you.

LET THE DOG BE OPERANT

Operant conditioning means that the dog is supposed to figure out what we want it to do. If, for instance, you want it to lie down, show the dog a treat or a toy and wait. The dog will now jump up at you, sit down, circle you, yelp and ... lie down. Now you must praise it and give it a treat.

This kind of learning is much more efficient than when you force or entice the dog to do something, because now the dog has to think and try to work out what to do. Clicker training is mainly based on the operant conditioning technique.

The more you train this way, the more the dog's ability to take the initiative increases.

Unhappy obedient dogs

You see these dogs everywhere; often they are dogs of a larger breed. They are very disciplined and walk close to their owners, held on a short leash. Dull eyes, ears back, tails pointed down and a slow walk. When

A dog should be allowed to choose where it wants to sniff and sometimes even the direction it wants to go. Don't forget: It's the dog's walk! (Photo: Shutterstock)

The freedom to run around and play is not reserved for small dogs. Big ones should be allowed to enjoy it as well. (Photo: Shutterstock)

I see these dog owners pass me on the sidewalk, I have always wondered why they remind me of drill sergeants. Perhaps they believe that it looks impressive to be in such control of a dog that it walks like a shadow beside you.

Some people have a need for and find satisfaction in being in total control over dogs – and also to show others that they are. They justify this by the fact that big dogs are so strong. They say that if a small dog jumps up on people or attacks other dogs, they are so easy to correct. You just have to hold on to the leash and pull the dog back.

It is different with a big and strong dog. If for instance a German Shepherd or a Rottweiler jumps up at a person, he or she may fall. If such a big dog attacks another dog it is more difficult to hold it back, the situation looks more dangerous and the dog can cause more damage.

EXAGGERATED OBEDIENCE

Of course, there is some truth to the fact that you need to be able to control a large dog more than a smaller one. However, that is beside the point. To be in total control over the dog and hold it on a short leash, even when there are no dogs or people around, is exaggerated obedience.

Unfortunately, there are seldom any limits to what the dog accepts when it comes to the owner's demands of obedience. Consequently, some dogs are exposed to unreasonable and exaggerated demands. They become pacified and more like robots and do nothing without a command from their master.

When you take a dog for a walk it is supposed to be able to sniff and pee without any stress, linger a moment by an interesting scent and look at the surroundings. Perhaps even greet another dog. It is the dog's walk, not a march for the dog owner to demonstrate obedience and control. Most small dogs get to do all of these things. They get to stop and sniff, pee as often as they want and often say hello to other dogs as well as people.

EXERCISING POWER

The worst form of obedience is when dog owners satisfy an inner need to exercise power, to dominate. It is in their hands that we find submissive dogs that are under constant restraint, and never allowed to take any initiatives of their own. They are not allowed to stop and pee or sniff when and where they want. Disobedience is perceived as a crime and therefore punished mercilessly. These dogs are constantly aware of the fact that their owner is watching them all the time just in case they dare to do something without permission. Their place is always by the owner's left side. Nowhere else.

A dog under this kind of pressure is extremely obedient and moves slowly, with tail hanging down, ears back and dull eyes. The dog owner looks satisfied, with his or her chin up, shoulders back and elbows slightly bent.

What you do not see is that the dog has paid a high price for the demands of this drill, and that the result is passivity and often fear of doing something wrong. Normally people do not see the background; instead, the skilled trainer impresses them. Consider how people react to TV programmes where an aggressive dog has changed to being kind and obedient in less than five minutes. You hear reactions such as "I never thought that was possible". But the viewers do not consider the price the dog has had to pay for this change ...

THERE IS ANOTHER WAY

A walk is so much more than just physical exercise or a chance to pee. A dog does not get exercise from just a short walk, and it does not fulfil its need for social interaction. What the dog needs, and what makes it feel content when you are getting home, are all those other things that happen during the walk, for instance a chance to investigate whether other dogs have been peeing in the area. For your dog, this is just like reading today's newspaper. To be able to squirt a few drops – "write" a message – is just as important as exercise. It is a social game, which makes the dog work mentally. This is the reason why exercising a dog on a treadmill or with your bike is not as efficient as walking.

Of course, you need to have more control over big dogs, but it does not mean that you have to use military discipline and prohibit any initiatives from the dog. A big dog should also be allowed to stop and sniff and pee, and perhaps choose in which direction to walk. It is, by the way, interesting to notice that dogs often prefer to walk against the wind.

I am always happy to see a big dog walking on a long leash and getting a bit of a mental workout from all the scents on the ground. Naturally, the big dog needs to come to heel when you pass a small, barking dog telling the big one that it will be beaten up if it comes too close...

It really warms my heart to see dog owners who give their dogs some mental exercise during the walk. Perhaps they hide a treat in the bark of a tree, have the dog search for keys that they "accidentally dropped", or ask it to jump up and balance on a rock, a tree trunk or a wall.

Instead of harsh voices, commands and pulling the leash, there are dog owners who reward their big dogs with praise and treats when they pass other dogs, children or disturbing things. This positive action means that the dog can feel in control.

It may experience the important feeling of taking the initiative and having some influence on its life.

"Natural fostering"

Some of those who prefer "hard" training use expressions such as "natural fostering" to defend their various dog training methods.

"You should do what the dog mother does and force the puppy to the ground. Wolf parents are very strict, you know." Some

Puppies and young dogs often play hunting games with a stick. (Photo: Shutterstock)

dog trainers use these comments to defend their hard training methods. These views are wrong – for both dogs and wolves – and other animals for that matter; none of them treat their offspring that way. On the contrary, their young are cared for, protected and defended if threatened.

The mother or father does not consciously use force on young animals. For the most part their children learn in two ways, by their own experience and by taking after other mature individuals in the group or the family.

Every action of a young animal results in an experience. If, for instance, it runs at full speed and stumbles, it will learn to watch out while running. If it bites somebody too hard during play, it will be bitten back equally hard. No parents are there to correct or punish the youngster.

If we look at wolves in the wild, we understand how important it is for their young to grow up with strong self-confidence. With less confidence, the youngest in the pack would not dare to attack big game that they know might turn and counterattack. This in turn could jeopardize the survival of the entire group. If the parents threaten and punish the cubs, they would become emotionally weak. Threat and punishment also lead to emotional responses such as fear and submission. The result would be that the young focus on the parents, not the prey or an enemy. Therefore, if the parents intervene and control their offspring's behaviour with threats or punishment, it lessens their own – and the whole pack's – chances of survival.

THE PUPPY'S PLAY – LEARNING BY TRIAL AND ERROR

When puppies reach a certain age – often as young as six weeks old – they learn how to hunt by chasing each other in wild play. They learn how to catch up, intercept, and anticipate movements in a fleeing "game" and how to throw each other to the ground. A young dog often challenges other dogs to a game of "hunting" with a stick in its mouth, as if he wanted to say, "Come on! Catch me if you can!"

This game, which is most common among puppies and young dogs, involves learning strategies that could later be used when hunting real game. You may see stealth and crawling, much like the position adopted before a sudden attack. A dog owner may very well see this during a walk with their dog. When it sees another dog it will lie flat on the ground, with its chin down as if it were hiding in high grass like a lion. It is impossible to get the dog to move. When the approaching dog is within two or three metres the "lion" will spring up like a jack-in-the-box. In this way the other dog is taken by surprise. Dogs that are uncertain in their relation to other dogs often use this strategy.

Puppies learn how to wrestle and fight with "prey" as well as with opponents of the same species. There are play-fighting games where they try to defeat an opponent by pinning it to the ground. In this game, you often hear growls and little barks used to strengthen a dog's position and intimidate its opponent.

Another game is a tug-of-war over a stick or similar. In this case, the dog is learning how to fight, not just to win. Some people warn against letting their dog win a tug-of-war because that would let the dog climb up a rung on the social ladder. Today we know that this is wrong. One such proof is that if the dog wins it immediately returns for a new game of tug-of-war.

LET PUPPIES BE PUPPIES

There are three unfortunate tendencies with regard to training puppies, namely too many rules, too many exercises, and too many or too few activities. People from the "hard" school are generally strict and set up rules right from day one. The puppy must not play or bite too much. Wild indoor games are not allowed; neither is greeting other dogs or jumping up on people. Protecting food or toys is also not allowed, and growling at people is a sin regardless of the reason, for instance if the puppy is afraid. Puppies raised in this manner will be insecure, submissive and often aggressive when they get older.

Determined and energetic people often become over-achievers when it comes to what their puppy should be able to perform. The puppy must learn as much as an adult dog and have as many activities as they do. The same kind of obsession can be seen in over-ambitious parents. We should not forget that puppies must be allowed to be puppies. Of course you should train them – but

it should be done playfully. And of course they should be stimulated – in moderation. Puppies also need a lot of rest.

However, it is more common that new dog owners, besides admiring the puppy, do nothing at all. There is no mental stimulation; there are no rules, no social or environmental training, no off-leash training and no coming when called. If too little time is devoted to the exercises needed for the puppy to adapt to the family and community, it may become socially handicapped. Without activities, which are of uttermost importance for brain development, the puppy's ability to cope with social and environmental disturbance and unfamiliar events is compromised.

A young dog's energy

Young dogs seem to be full of mischief. This is a time when many dog owners feel they have a problem dog – because the puppy is so wild. They pull on the leash, bark, chew on things, do not come when you call, jump up on people, fight with other dogs, chase after animals and joggers and do not listen at all.

This is not a behavioural problem. It is just energy and exuberance!

Therefore, such behaviour should not be met with discipline, correction, punishment and control. That would turn the young dog's energy into passivity and suppress its exuberance until it fades into

Puppies should be allowed to be just puppies and have their own experiences. (Photo: Maurer)

melancholy. The result will be a dog that is unable to do anything without an order, a dog that is afraid to take any form of initiative, resulting in an empty soul and a dull look. The puppy becomes an old dog much too soon.

DO NOT TRAIN THE SYMPTOMS – ADDRESS THE CAUSE

Do not listen to advice about correcting problems with punishment and control. Do not listen to those who call the dog's intensity "bad behaviour". Do not listen to advice on how to "put the dog in its place", or show it who is the boss and leader. Do not let yourself be fooled by experts who tell you to go against the nature of the dog, and to inflict any kind of discomfort to make it stop certain behaviours. All such advice is just meant to stop the symptoms.

The cause of the problem is excess energy! This is why the young dog may have trouble listening and is sometimes difficult to handle. Therefore, you have to handle it as an energy problem rather than a problem of disobedience, bad behaviour or your bad "leadership". It is a delicate balancing act between coming to terms with what feels hard to deal with in your young dog or letting it keep the exuberance and ability to take the initiative. After all, your dog is your best friend so of course you want it to be happy.

An effective way of channelling your dog's energy is with mental activation. Thereby you can establish a good relationship without any conflicts (15). And best of

all, your dog will not become passive and sad, but keep its exuberance and ability to communicate.

Punishment, correction and reprimand

Today there are dog programmes on TV that demonstrate how to correct problem behaviour by punishing dogs. They just use other words for it, and claim that correcting and disciplining the dog is not the same as punishing it. However, all negative action intended to stop a behaviour is punishment by definition.

TO PUNISH OR NOT?

Most people think that negative consequences resulting from an action will teach the individual not to repeat the action. This is true, if certain preconditions are met, namely that:

· It is the first time for the behaviour, for instance when a dog steals food from the table.
· The motivation is low, the dog is not hungry, it is just tempted by food on the table.
· The negative consequence occurs immediately when the behaviour starts, for example at precise second the dog jumps up on the table.

How often will you find these preconditions when you say "No!" or "Bad dog!" or pull on the leash and slap the dog? The

Too late! Punishments don't work, especially not when they do not occur immediately after the behaviour has just started. (Photo: Shutterstock)

answer is: not often. This means that most punishments do not result in any change in the behaviour other than just temporarily.

However, what many do not realize is that when you punish a dog, things happen to your relationship. If a dog perceives its owner as dominating, controlling and punishing, it will become submissive and passive, and it may develop all sorts of behavioural problems. An interesting example was found in a Dutch study, where they noticed a higher level of the stress hormone cortisol in dogs that had been treated harshly (32).

SOME PUNISHMENTS HAVE LASTING RESULTS, BUT ...

When a negative consequence of an action is very strong, that is, when the punishment is very severe, then a dog might stop doing the forbidden act for a long time. However, you have scared the dog, perhaps shocked it, and this leads to other consequences. The dog will be scared of the punisher and often show strong signs of submission as soon as the person raises their voice to anyone. The dog becomes passive and dares not take the initiative. It will more easily develop aggression towards other dogs, which in turn results in further punishment. In time, the dog may show a variety of stress symptoms, such as stomach problems and a weakened immune system making it more prone to disease.

If you interpret the animal welfare policies and protection laws correctly, you cannot abuse or hurt a dog. Furthermore, it is unethical. If you are not able to teach a dog to refrain from certain things without frightening or hurting it, then you need to work on your training skills. There are so many positive ways to train a dog!

If you have to punish the dog for the same problem behaviour time after time, without any lasting result, then you really need to stop and think. If I have to keep taking my car to the repair shop for the same work, over and over again, then I know that there is something wrong with the car mechanic. If my child keeps doing the same thing numerous times, even if I say no, then I realize that I have to find an alternative way of dealing with the problem.

To achieve a permanent change, you need to reward the dog when it refrains from doing something. This means that you must have quick reflexes. If the dog attacks other dogs, you must reward the dog immediately when it spots another dog and before it shows signs of wanting to attack it. When you practise this, you need to keep a distance from other dogs and then gradually make this smaller. The best way is to train to meet other dogs, perhaps every day for a certain period. Advance the training by small steps.

It is essential to change your own behaviour, above all your temper, so that you do not appear aggressive in the eyes of the dog. It is easy to understand that aggression does not help in learning. It only creates fear. I have noticed that there are around forty ways to punish a dog, but only five or six ways to reward it ...

Make the walk exciting

You are taking the dog for a walk and then you start talking on your mobile phone. There is no traffic around and no other dogs in sight, so you let the dog run free. You have full control... Then in a split second it happens – a scared hare jumps up in front of you and the dog starts chasing it.

There is nothing more boring than a dog owner who is preoccupied with talking on the phone during a walk. Zero contact and zero control! This means that the dog can do what it wants – and that is exactly what it will do. It wants to have some fun and excitement during the walk.

Perhaps you are careful and keep an eye on the surroundings, so that the dog does not chase after an animal or a jogger. Your ears and eyes are registering the surroundings. But the dog does the same and is bored, because just sniffing on old and new stuff is not particularly exciting.

So you and your dog carefully observe what is happening around you. Now the walk has become a question of who has the best sense of smell, eyesight and hearing. Who can make the quickest start and run fastest? You or the dog? Guess who ...

TIPS FOR AN INTERESTING WALK

It is possible to prevent and cure problems with a dog that wants to run up to other dogs, or chase after animals, joggers or other moving objects.

Step one: Avoid using your mobile phone during walks. Do not engage in other personal things during this time. Make sure you are part of the team, which is you and your dog.

Step two: Divide the walk into several stations, where the dog gets some mental stimulation with a fun assignment, a different one in every "station". You will be able to find suggestions for activities from these four categories: nose work, learning new things, problem-solving and balance. In one place, perhaps the dog can search for treats in the bark of a tree or on the ground. At stop two, it has to learn a new

During walks you can find a lot of opportunities to stimulate your dog mentally. (Photo: Maurer)

Most dogs pull on the leash to release energy. (Photo: Shutterstock)

trick. At stop three, it must figure out how to move sticks around to get to a toy, and at stop four, it is challenged to balance on a fallen tree. You will be able to find more ideas for mental stimulation in books, for example my book "Mental Activation" (15).

The distance between the different stations may vary. In the beginning, they should be relatively short, perhaps fifty to a hundred metres. If you have a problem letting the dog run free during walks the distances between stations should be shorter, otherwise they can be longer.

It normally takes only a few days for the dog to lose interest in running away during walks, because now you are providing all the variety and excitement he seeks. From now on the dog is looking forward to where the next activity station could be. Suddenly it has an intense contact with you and wants to hurry to the next fun and exciting place.

Full speed ahead — pulling on the leash

Of all problem behaviours there is none surrounded by so much advice and suggested training methods as pulling on the leash. Most of these ideas are just uncomfortable for the dog and just discouraging quick fixes aimed at dealing with the behaviour.

Dogs, especially young ones, have a lot of energy. The dog as a species is not lazy, it is actually a workaholic. In young dogs, it is a question of curiosity, exuberance, enthusiasm and a lot of energy. No wonder then that they are in a hurry the moment they step out the door, especially during their morning walk after resting all night and with their legs full of restlessness.

Dogs have a remarkable capacity to adapt, which is both good and bad. They completely adapt to our way of life. In addition, it is programmed into their system to synchronize their behaviour with their family. This is similar to how wolves in a wolf family are coordinated when resting or being active.

This means that your dog will be calm at home and release its built up energy during walks. Indoors it will do what we do and relax. The dog thinks that we are really boring. Therefore, it will go and sleep somewhere waiting for a chance to get outside and have some fun.

As if this is not enough, we make the dog even more passive with the training methods mentioned earlier. They focus mostly on suppressing and calming the young wild dog so that it does not "misbehave" by jumping on people, barking, yelping, chewing on things, chasing animals and people and wanting to run towards every dog they meet.

We think that the training has been successful when we have a calm, obedient and passive dog, which means a dog that is not wild indoors and not troublesome outdoors. But is this success?

IT IS A QUESTION OF ENERGY

When the dog is "calm and nice" at home, lies still and sleeps, it builds up energy. When the dog is then taken out for a walk, it has a lot of excess energy. This is the reason why the dog pulls on the leash! Other behavioural problems may also be due to excess energy, which is why many feel they are so difficult to handle.

Dogs are workaholics and if they only get a chance to release energy for an hour or two a day, is it any wonder that they pull on the leash?

The dog pulls most intensely at the beginning of the walk, because then it has a build-up of energy. Usually the dogs pulls less on the way back, after having used up some of that excess energy.

Therefore, to be fair to the dog, you should work on the cause – the energy – not the symptom, in this case pulling on the leash. If you do this, you can disregard all of those suggestions that only lead to hurting or scaring the dog to get them to walk nicely.

When I was young, there was a man in my neighbourhood who seemed so lonely and depressed. Whenever I saw him, I felt sorry for him. However, one day he seemed like a new man. I found out that he had adopted a Norwegian Elkhound. This strong dog pulled him along like a sled dog. He was out for hours with his new friend, smiling happily. The dog seemed happy too. After just a couple of days, I noticed that the dog had stopped pulling so hard on the leash. And I knew that no trainer had been involved in that. The simple answer was that the dog got all the exercise it needed.

THE SOLUTION

The first advice I give regarding a dog that pulls on the leash is to start stimulating it physically and mentally. For instance, you can let the dog search for treats, or open packages fifteen to twenty minutes before the walk. Dog owners who followed this advice told me that the dogs pulled less on the leash or had stopped altogether sometimes even the same day.

Some dog owners want their dogs to walk to heel during their walk, which of course is wrong and certainly no fun for the dog. It should only need to heel when you cross a road or when you wish to avoid meeting other dogs or people. It is the dog's walk, not yours, so the dog should be able to walk the entire length of the leash and enjoy the small amount of freedom we can give it.

When you ask the dog not to pull on the leash you have to act quickly, without sounding angry and commanding – you never have to. At the exact second the dog starts to pull, say very softly "not like that", and stop for a couple of seconds. Then give the dog a long leash and continue walking while you praise it.

The dog does not understand that pulling on the leash is wrong. In order to teach the dog to understand this, you need exercises where it is rewarded when it walks nicely. For this exercise, pick a stretch of five to ten metres, depending on the size of your dog. This stretch is your training area. Walk back and forth until the dog stops pulling. If you have stimulated the dog physically and mentally before training, the desired result will soon come.

Then pick a new stretch and repeat the exercise. If things are progressing, you can take a little longer walk every time. Your praise should sound nice, almost like a song. After a few days, you will notice a big difference.

Of course, you should allow your dog to pull lightly, for example in the direction of an interesting smell it wants to investigate. What you want to get rid of is the constant hard pulling or lunging at the leash.

Do not forget old dogs!

The puppy period is so special – both wonderful and sometimes a little inconvenient. The first year also has its special activities. There are classes and training in this and that. Young dogs have no problem with other dogs, and they can accompany you almost everywhere. Life is fun and in high gear.

Soon this time has passed, but there are still many activities available such as competitions, taking classes for tracking, searching and other skills. Still everything is lots of fun.

Being calm at home is not a sign of old age. The dog is just synchronizing its activities with the rest of the group, as mentioned earlier. As the grey hairs increase the dog stops expecting and insisting on some activity. That does not mean that they do not need it! Perhaps you feel that you do not have enough time and that the walks are sufficient. But they are far from enough!

Senior dogs are not retired, they still love to be active and "work". (Photo: Shutterstock)

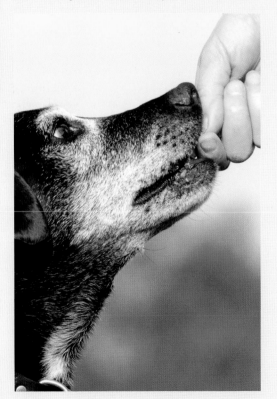

Dogs age slowly and have a lot of energy that they need to use in physical and mental activities. They are not old until they really are old. So their physical and mental capacity does not fade as gradually as you may think. No animal species would survive for very long if their capacity and energy did not remain for as long as possible. "Old" should come as late as possible in life.

CLASSES FOR SENIORS ARE COMING

When the dog is around six or eight there are no more classes left to take. Some dog owners are still active with their dogs in competitions – these are the lucky dogs. However, the choices of interesting activities for older dogs from clubs and private trainers are very few, if not non-existent. The older the dog gets, the emptier its life becomes. "Retirement age" for most of them means sleeping or resting for the rest of their life. This is not right!

Now we are starting to see classes for senior dogs. They are much needed. These classes do not ask too much of the old dog, and they are adapted to the old dog's much needed mental and physical stimulation. Often there are massage therapists involved in these classes and sometimes a veterinarian who checks the dogs.

Those who have tried these classes all say that they are wonderful for trainers and dog owners as well as the older dogs. These seniors become like puppies again, to their owners' delight.

Activate your senior!

Dealing with
A PROBLEM DOG

More than half of all dog owners in western societies seek advice about dog problems. Many offer their services in this area, from amateurs to qualified trainers, animal behaviourists to dog psychologists. However, they all have different views on how to deal with problem behaviour, which means that you need to be discerning when seeking help. If someone gives you advice based on punishment and dominance it is my recommendation not to listen to them. However, if the advice is focused on finding the causes behind the problem behaviour it is a more constructive way to find a permanent solution. Statistics from several countries show that approximately half of all dog owners experience problems with their dogs. It can be everything from a dog barking too much, to pulling on the leash or even wanting to attack people. There are as many dog problems as letters of the alphabet – and four times as much advice.

Columns in dog magazines are filled with suggestions on how to correct problem behaviour and most dog books have chapters with methods on how to train dogs to get rid of the problem. Experts, friends, neighbours and programmes on TV also willingly give advice.

However, what most of them have in common is that they focus on training to cure the symptoms, for instance excessive

(Photo: Shutterstock)

barking. Typically, suggestions include various forms of punishment, ranging from squirting water in a dog's face to more brutal methods such as punching it, as well as pulling hard on the leash and even the use of electric collars.

A DOG PSYCHOLOGIST'S APPROACH

One thing is for sure, a dog psychologist would not start any training prematurely. First, we would look at the problem behaviour as a symptom and then start investigating to find out the causes behind the problem. We would carry out several tests as well as observing the dog in various situations. Then we make an analysis.

There are so many reasons why a dog may end up exhibiting problem behaviour. It might be under-stimulated or have muscle pain. Perhaps it has bad eyesight.

A dog psychologist would never include "bad leadership" in a diagnosis. There are two reasons why: first, a dog owner is almost never too gentle – often it is the other way around. Second, to diagnose the dog's problem as a result of your own "bad leadership" is neither constructive nor ethical. It only leads to even harsher handling and control of the dog under the guise of "increased leadership".

There are so many other reasons behind problem behaviour. The most common causes are under-stimulation, over-stimulation, pain, hormone imbalances and post-traumatic stress (PTS). Many dog owners also add to the problem by responding with punishment.

Shy dogs

Forty years ago, the common belief was that if dogs were shy, wary of people or afraid of strangers they were mentally "bad". I was always surprised when dog owners came to me for help with dogs that they said were scared, shy or angry when they met people.

The thing was that the same dogs almost never reacted in a shy way to my assistants or me. The dog owners did not understand it and scratched their heads.

"That's just typical! When I come here my dog does not show how he really is!"

I found none of these dogs to be scared or angry. They only reacted to people's threatening body signals. These begin at a distance. The first mistake is to establish steady eye contact with the dog (threat). Then to go straight up to the dog (threat). Then bend over the dog (threat). Then pat the dog on the forehead near the eyes (threat). And finally, show them a friendly smile with a row of white teeth (threat).

These signals are not a problem if they come from people the dog already knows, such as family members. However, when strange people show these signals the dog might misinterpret them and then the problems start.

If everyone knew how to act correctly when meeting dogs, I do not think there would be many scared, shy or aggressive dogs. If you are aware of the body signals that may be perceived as threatening for the dog, you can just change that in your body language.

Dogs may feel threatened when a stranger pats them on the forehead near the eyes. (Photo: Shutterstock)

· Avoid eye contact.
· Do not walk straight up to the dog; aim at a spot beside it.
· Stop at a short distance from the dog and hunch down with your face turned away. (This is especially important if it is a small dog.)

With this approach the dog may decide whether it wants to say hello – and most dogs will want to, because you are being so nice and polite. Then, when you pet the dog, do it on the cheeks or under the chin. Do not pat a dog on the forehead near the eyes. Now you have a new friend!

Over-stimulation

A common misconception is that over-stimulation may be a result of your dog being involved in too many activities. However, that would only happen if the dog did not get any rest or relaxation at all between those activities. If this really were the case, you would have to keep your dog busy for many hours every day. No dog owner would have enough energy or time for that.

Over-stimulation means that the dog has to work hard physically so frequently that its stress system never gets a chance to recuperate. For the body to be able to cope with physical and mental hard work, nerve impulses need to stimulate the adrenal glands to release stress hormones. For shorter periods of hard work, adrenaline and noradrenaline are released. For longer periods, or periods of repeated stress, the stress hormone cortisol will increase in the blood (14).

The most important task for stress hormones is to strengthen the muscles by adding "fuel" in the form of blood sugar, oxygen and fat.

· Blood sugar is released from the liver.
· Increased breathing raises the level of oxygen.
· Fat is released from fat depots throughout the body.
· Extra blood is "borrowed" from the stomach area and released into the muscles.

All of this together nearly doubles the muscle strength of the body. You can run faster, fight harder and lift heavier things. This has always been important for the dog's wild cousin, the wolf, to be able to catch and overpower their prey. Dogs are very similar to the wolf and, in this case, they function in the same way.

GAMES DOGS PLAY

Every time you throw a stick or a ball for your dog and let it run after it the situation can be compared to chasing after prey. When you play-fight with your dog it is the same as wrestling with prey. When dogs play "hunter and prey"" in wild chasing games or wrestle with each other they are also mimicking what happens in the wild. And in all of these cases, stress hormones are released.

Dogs love these kinds of games, because they are natural for them. The stress reaction that inevitably occurs during wild games will go away after a few moments of rest.

However, here is the snag. Hunting-induced stress reactions happen more seldom in the wild, because it is hard to find prey. It also depends on the season. During spring and early summer, wolves kill a lot of small game. In these times is easy to find food, and they do not have to work too hard for it. During the winter, they have to watch out for bigger game and work much harder while hunting, but it does not happen so often. Overall, their stress system is adapted to fit their living conditions. Our domestic dogs have similar genes, but different living conditions.

If you let the dog play long and hard every single day, the stress system never gets a chance to recover. The dog will have an increased level of stress hormones and you risk having a dog with behavioural problems. Depending on the kind of wild play, the dog may need up to two days before the body has recuperated.

Of course your dog should be allowed to play a little wildly now and then with you or with friends in the dog park. The most important thing is to have in mind not to overdo it.

Under-stimulation

The notion that dogs can be under-stimulated occurred to me for the first time in the early 1970s. A couple came to me for advice regarding their three-year-old male Samoyed. This dog went too far with everything he did. First, his greeting was overjoyed, and then he started to ride my leg and bite me, playfully at first, but then harder and harder.

Finally, I asked them to remove him before the scene turned bloody. And the dog was not angry! He was just intense. I did not understand how he could have all this energy. I asked the owners how long the dog was taken for walks every day. "All in all, about an hour" was the answer.

Wild chasing games are fun, but this kind of play also releases stress hormones. (Photo: Shutterstock)

The dog jumped about and would not calm down, so I suggested that we should take a walk. I then tried to find out more about the dog's daily activities.

"Is your garden fenced in?" I asked.

"No, we do not have a garden, we live in an apartment," they replied.

Then I started to think. This dog did not get enough exercise. That was obvious. But what else did they offer him in order to channel all this energy?

No garden, well then... activities indoors perhaps? I kept asking questions.

"How much do you play with your dog at home?"

"At home? There I have only one principle and one command, which is: Go to your bed!" was the answer.

Then it hit me. This dog was not allowed to be active indoors; he had to use all his energy outside. A quick calculation told me that the dog was active only for about an hour plus a few minutes for eating, greeting any visitors or walking to the door to go outside. I wrote a note in my journal: "1.5 hours of activity per day".

The calculation is easy. Out of the day's 24 hours, the Samoyed had 1.5 hours of activity. For the remaining 22.5 hours, he was forced to be passive.

No wonder that the dog was over-energetic and unable to control himself. When he finally had a chance to do something he exploded! When I explained this to the couple, they went pale when they realized what the cause of the problem was. We immediately set up an activation programme. They would activate the dog both with long walks and various activities at home to stimulate him mentally. The dog was "cured" after a week.

THROW YOUR PRINCIPLES IN THE WASTEBASKET

There seems to be a strange phenomenon with many dog owners – they establish principles. The dog must not sleep on the bed or on the couch. It cannot be near the dining table when you are eating nor jump up and greet people. During its walks, it is not allowed to sniff for too long on other dogs' pee spots or greet strange dogs, and it is also not allowed to stop and pee as often as it wants.

Well, these principles are seldom good for dogs. Of course, dogs have to behave so they don't irritate people, but many dog owners go too far. Therefore, if you belong to the group with hard principles I suggest you start questioning your rules. Dogs have such a short life, and we should be able to afford them a little more freedom and fewer restrictions. Principles are also often unnecessary. So what if the dog sleeps on the couch? You can put a blanket where the dog wants to be. So what if the dog is a little wild and rambunctious and runs around happily in the house so that dust and carpets fly? You can clean and straighten the carpets. Let the dog play in all of the rooms. It will not damage your furniture. So what if the dog is nearby when you sit at the dinner table? If you do not want it to beg, give it a bone or something else to chew on.

There is nothing wrong with a dog relaxing on the sofa – if it's ok with you. (Photo: Shutterstock)

YOUR DOG IS A FAMILY MEMBER

Just like their ancestors the wolves, our domestic dogs are genetically programmed to live in family packs, and be active together with the other members of their group. This means that friendships, company, socializing, being cosy together and being able to cooperate with each other are all natural needs, which should be fulfilled.

Therefore, it is important for us to understand that being active together with the family is part of being a dog. So in addition to long daily walks that should be a matter of course, let the dog accompany you on short errands, for instance to the laundry room or taking the garbage out.

These are small inspirations in an otherwise dull day for the dog. If a dog's needs are fulfilled, it will be naturally tired and mellow. Again, there are several books with suggestions or tips on how to give your dog more mental stimulation, for example my book "Mental Activation" (15).

Boredom – the agony of all dogs

Dogs that are bored, or in other words under-stimulated, tend to develop destructive and annoying behaviour such as barking, chewing on shoes, jumping up on people and other things. Long-term periods of under-stimulation can lead to depression and apathy. Studies on rats showed that the cortex of the brain shrank when the animals were exposed to under-stimulation. In rats that were stimulated the cortex grew (7).

The result of my Swedish study showed that nearly 75 percent of the country's dogs were under-stimulated (14). These pets rested for at least twenty hours per day. Problem behaviours were more common with those dogs than with dogs that had more active lives.

Dogs are genetically programmed for a social life but they depend on others in their to take the initiative. When no one in the family initiates any activity, they just rest and wait for something to happen.

In an ordinary human family where members perhaps are gone for most of the day, the dog spends its days resting and waiting for someone to come home and start activities. Often there is not much time when you come home after work. We have other things to do; the activity might just be a dutiful walk. Then the dog is left to rest again. The "square things" in the home are the dog's worst enemy: the newspaper, the TV and the computer. After that comes our occupation with cleaning, cooking and various outdoor activities and hobbies. The time left for the dog may shrink to a minimum. And the dog waits and waits ...

NATURAL PASSIVITY

Dogs are passive by nature because their energy is supposed to be at the service of the group. Among wild canines,

Dogs love to learn tricks. (Photo: Shutterstock)

automatic coordination takes place and everybody in the group rests and is active at the same time. In this way they are all rested and full of energy when needed for a hunt or a long hike. It would never work if some individuals were tired and some rested when the group had to work hard. This is the reason why our dogs rest and wait if we do not stimulate them.

When the dog gets too active, perhaps barking, playing too wildly in a burst of energy, chewing on things and showing signs of energy peaks, most people try to calm and "correct" it. This means that, through training, we force the dog to become passive. In time, it learns how to be "well behaved", which means to be quiet, remain still and wait, and I wait ...

CAN IT BE TOO MUCH?

It is our responsibility to satisfy the dog's need for activity. Taking a walk is great, but not enough. The dog also needs mental stimulation, and there are plenty of classes around. Some people may warn you that you might stress your dog with too much mental activation and physical activity. If that was the case, it would take far too much time out of any dog owner's life.

However, there can be risks for dogs that spend their days at a dog daycare centre. If the dog is stimulated a lot during the day in the centre, it might be too much if the owner also activates it in the evening. If your dog seems to be tired, you should of course let it rest.

Risk groups are people with too much ambition, for instance those who compete with their dogs or really overdo those fun activities. However, the over-achievers are few. The biggest problem is still that too many dogs rest for too many hours per day.

THE ADVANTAGES OF MENTAL STIMULATION

Mental activation stimulates the frontal lobes, positioned at the most forward part of the brain, where we find most of our cognitive functions. We use these when we think, work things out, try to understand and learn things.

Thoughts and feelings are symbolically on the opposite sides of the scale. The more you think, the more inhibited your emotions are, and vice versa. The stronger the emotions are, the less you are able to think clearly and figure things out. You might recall all those instances where you were upset and could not think clearly. Once you had calmed down, you knew what you should have said or done.

It is the same with the dog. Strong feelings "block" the dog's brain. It does not listen. It does not learn and cannot relax. By stimulating the brain's primary cognitive centre, the frontal lobes, with mental activation you may help the dog control its feelings. This is, for instance, an important part of any therapy when teaching a dog to be less scared of something.

Come rain or shine

The weather is nice, the sky is blue, there are a few clouds and some sunshine and the temperature is comfortable. It is a perfect day to take your dog for a walk. Grab some treats and the poop bag and out we go. It is really fun and easy to have a dog. However, when the weather is bad, when it is very windy, raining or snowing, it is a nightmare to think about having to go out in that mud and rain. In addition, you have to put all those thick clothes on. You forget the poop bag and the treats and the dog is eagerly pulling on the leash. Now many cannot help but feel that it is a burden having a dog.

Regardless of the weather the dog must go outside – that is where the toilet is. And most of its daily activities are outside – physical exercise, smells, meeting other dogs and a variety of experiences. You knew from the start that one of the dog's basic rights was to be able to go out. And it is your duty to make sure that the dog gets its daily walks.

Just like you, the dog might not be too crazy about stepping out in the rain. If the dog hates bad weather, you might want to get it a raincoat. However, some dogs do not seem to care at all if they get wet. Walks tend to get shorter in bad weather, which is quite all right, but then you need to compensate and stimulate the dog at home.

EXERCISE MAKES DOGS FEEL GOOD

Exercise is like medicine. Doctors even prescribe it nowadays. It is good for everybody to exercise, not just dogs. It releases endorphins, which make you feel good in addition to being an analgesic. It is a fact that exercise can help cure bad backs, prevent heart and vascular disorders, increase the absorption of nutrients and improve the immune system. It leads to a better quality of life and a longer lifespan.

Sadly, our dogs are unable to protest and demand their right to the walks that they need to feel good. They are so willing to adapt that they just accept longer rests at home and the lack of physical and mental stimulation. As a result, many dogs develop a surplus of energy which results in problem behaviour.

If you feel that you cannot give the dog enough time for outdoor walks, perhaps you should think about giving the dog to a family who has the time and energy to

Even if it may be hard ...

Daily exercise is obligatory. Your own comfort must never be more important than the dog's needs!

When the weather is nice, activities outside are really fun. (Photo: Shutterstock)

fulfil the dog's needs. There are of course alternatives such as doggy daycare centres or hiring someone to help you walk the dog, perhaps a teenager or a retired person. Many people like to do this as an extra job.

Dangerous dog collars

It has become a tradition for many dog owners to use a collar and leash to keep their dogs under control. More and more dog training classes have appeared since the 1950s, and the most common method to teach the dog to obey was by using hard jerks on the leash. Soon, choke collars were available on the market. People believed that they were a more efficient tool to force the dog to obey. The thought was that dogs learned to obey quicker if they were exposed to pain, that is, if you hurt them. Jerks on the leash soon became the most common method and were used in all forms of training. Little did people realize that it was, and is, a bad training method, which may be truly damaging for the dog.

NECK AND THROAT – SENSITIVE AREAS

Early in my work with problem dogs, I noticed that injuries and disease were often the real cause behind their problem behaviour. This realization led to my collaboration with physiotherapists in the 1970s, and this quickly grew. Many of these experts pointed out that collars were risky and in fact bad for dogs – in particular the choke collar.

Injuries to the cervical vertebrae, in the neck area, are common if the dog owner, or the dog, pulls hard on the leash. In my study from 1994, it was found that one quarter of the dogs suffered from neck damage (11). Soon more disturbing facts were revealed. The Norwegian veterinarian Are Thoresen examined the necks of 350 dogs that came to his clinic for various reasons. He found that 78 percent of these dogs had injuries to their necks and almost all of them wore collars (34).

As an experiment, press hard against your own throat, and then perhaps you will understand how it feels for a dog when a collar is pressing hard against its throat. It is even worse with a choke collar. This area is extremely sensitive and I cannot help but wonder how many cases of tracheal collapse (the trachea is the windpipe) have been caused by the repeated pressure of a collar.

When a collar presses hard on the neck, the muscles tense in a reflex response. This is particularly evident with the use of choke collars, which expose several muscles to pressure. The increased tension blocks normal blood flow to the brain. When it happens to you and me, we end up with a "tension" headache. Dogs most probably feel the same. There are several reported cases where a dog's problem behaviour subsided or vanished when a harness was used instead of a collar, and the dog was given a massage around the neck.

There are sensitive nerves embedded behind and between the muscles in the neck and throat. When the muscles are subjected to heavy or repeated pressure, they can swell and irritate these underlying nerves. The most sensitive of these is the trigeminal, a nerve with endings in three places in the face. To put pressure on this nerve can result in excruciating pain.

The thyroid gland sits on either side of the windpipe, below the larynx (voice box). There is a suspicion that the pressure of a collar, especially a choke collar, may damage it. The reason for this is not yet fully understood (36). In one study, people who had been in car accidents were examined (8). It was found that because of the seat belt's position across the neck it could cause damage to the thyroid gland. Dog collars press against the same area, which therefore could be a risk factor.

Strong pulls can cause whiplash injuries, regardless of the type of collar. In this respect, dogs are as sensitive as humans are. It has to do with how heavy the head is in proportion to the length of the neck and how violent the jerk is.

Pressure around the throat and neck increases eye pressure temporarily. For dogs that pull on the leash, or if you pull or jerk, this repeated pressure might eventually hurt the dog's eyes (30). Dogs with eye disease, or those that have had surgery on one or both eyes, should definitely not wear collar. They should wear a harness instead.

THE HIGH COLLAR – A CRUEL TECHNIQUE

In dog programmes on television, it has become more and more common to see trainers place a thin collar high up behind the dog's ears. With such a collar, jerking on the leash will really hurt the dog. This is the reason why it is seen as more "efficient". Nevertheless, to train dogs by hurting them is not acceptable, especially from an ethical point of view. If the muscles in this area swell up it may result in chronic pain for the dog.

Furthermore, this kind of thin collar sits closer to the thin hyoid bone (the lingual bone) behind the throat, which can snap if the leash is jerked or pulled too hard.

Dogs should wear a harness instead of a collar.
(Photo: Maurer)

Puppies should be allowed to run free and play with other dogs so that they can learn how to interact socially. (Photo: Shutterstock)

JERKING ON THE LEASH IS DANGEROUS

The centuries-old method that involves training dogs by pulling on the leash does not seem to want to disappear, despite all the evidence against it that has been available for almost two decades. Instead, the method seems to have received a boost from many dog programmes on TV. Many dog clubs and trainers are still using this outdated training method. People who recommend it do not acknowledge that it can be dangerous.

Jerks on the leash are a quick-fix method of training, but this is a bad and potentially dangerous practice. Collars are not good for dogs! A harness is clearly a much better choice (3, 11). We need to spread the word about how to train dogs without pulling and jerking.

Dogs that do not like other dogs

It used to be relatively uncommon that dogs attacked or showed other signs of aggression towards other dogs, but today it is a very common problem behaviour. This is what the majority of dog owners are seeking help for from dog psychologists and trainers. You cannot help but wonder why.

Some do not trust their dogs to be near other dogs. They are afraid that the dog will attack and bite. Others, on the other hand, are afraid that their own dog will be attacked, frightened or bullied by other dogs. Sadly, there are aggressive dogs around and sometimes they have owners who disregard others' safety and let their dogs run loose.

EARLY SOCIAL TRAINING

Unfortunately, many puppies are not allowed to run free with other dogs. There are even puppy classes where the young dogs may not run free, play together or learn how to socialize in a good way. It is of crucial importance that the puppy learns how to interact socially.

However, it is also important that no adult dog intimidates the puppy. There are of course those who claim that it is natural for both a mother dog and other older dogs to wrestle puppies to the ground to teach them submission. This is also a misconception regarding wolves. But it is wrong! It is not natural and it is not good. The way a puppy is treated by other dogs and humans will reflect how it treats dogs and humans later in life (5, 18).

POSSIBLE CAUSES

In countries where you see dogs running free, dogfights are unusual. Take for instance many southern European countries where dogs roam around free. Their social interaction is for the most part without conflict.

In general, our dogs are kept on a leash. Unfortunately, this may lead to an increased risk of aggression. When dogs are regularly stopped from greeting other dogs, they get frustrated. Eventually, this frustration may grow into anger directed towards all dogs they meet.

With you at the other end of the leash, the dog feels that you are supporting its "criminal" behaviour. If you shout, jerk or pull on the leash then its stress level is at a maximum. Police dogs are trained in a similar way. They are held back with a firm grip on the collar while their handler shouts and excites the dog against a figurant pretending to be aggressive.

Another cause of aggression is pain. Most animals have no means of showing you that they are in pain, and it is of course the same with dogs. However, it is more common than you may think that your pet is likely to be suffering from some sort of pain, and unfortunately chronic pain is especially hard to discover.

Trouble related to the locomotor apparatus, that is, the muscles, joints and the back, is most common. The probability of a dog ending up with back problems is about the same as it is for human beings, about 60 percent. For dogs, the cause is often minor muscle injuries from rough games or accidents (11).

DO NOT FOCUS ON SYMPTOMS

If someone offers to help you with problem behaviour and then starts punishing the dog for the symptoms, in this case the problem behaviour, then I must warn you. The dog will only behave better temporarily. If the correction is severe enough you risk ending up with a passive, submissive and unhappy dog. Unfortunately, there are certain programmes on TV that advocate punishment as the way to change a dog's behaviour. That is why we now see dog owners who punish their dogs more or less unrestrainedly and exert their authority on them. To train the symptoms, the behavioural problem, without identifying and addressing the cause is not only inefficient but also unethical.

Small and large dogs can be good friends. (Photo: Shutterstock)

Problems between small and large dogs

It is true that small dogs often bark more and may seem tougher and cockier than larger dogs, but the reason for this is not what you might think. For small dogs, almost everybody else is much bigger and they feel inferior. Those who are "cocky" and seem challenging are really just insecure and afraid deep inside, which can be true for both dogs and humans. They do not trust others and therefore they try to gain respect by showing that they certainly would not back off if threatened. They try to be one step ahead and intimidate and discourage other dogs from challenging them. You should never force a small dog to greet other dogs. It would only make it more frightened and uncertain.

The worst thing you can do is punish a small dog when it barks at a larger dog, because then you rob the little dog of its only way of taking a defensive stand.

Instead, you should stop and calm the dog, give it an extra treat and ask the dog owner with the bigger dog to keep it at a distance. Soon your small dog realizes that it does not have to be worried. If a large dog is loose and comes running towards you, you should shoo it away, or even better toss a few treats at it. In most cases it will stop to search for the treats on the ground.

It is best to plan this training and arrange to have the small dog play and socialize with a larger, but very calm and nice dog. Ideally, it should be a dog that really does not pay much attention to the smaller one. You should take enough long walks together in order for them to become friends. Then you can repeat this with another friendly big dog. After that, it is usually much easier for the small dog to accept bigger dogs. When the little dog has made some bigger friends it can be let loose to play with them, but only if the big dogs do not play too roughly. Small dogs can easily get hurt in rough games.

Barking too much

My dog and I had just crossed the main road and turned onto a quiet side street when a car slowed down before the intersection. I heard an excited barking from inside the car and the whole car actually seemed to be rocking from the commotion inside. A big dog was barking and throwing itself against the windows, apparently trying to get to my dog. I heard the owner shouting in a threatening way to quiet his dog down.

When a dog is upset, its brain is blocked from incoming stimuli. Loud, excited sounds, like yelling, may slip through, but only in primitive form. What might slip through reaches the so-called limbic system, the emotional centre of the brain. These shouting voices will only increase a dog's stress reaction. Therefore, by shouting at your dog you just add fuel to the fire.

Again, it is pointless to try to change problem behaviour by punishment-based quick-fix methods, whatever is said on some popular dog programmes on TV or in books.

BARKING IN THE CAR

It is not difficult to teach the dog not to bark in the car. You just have to plan a training programme built on rewarding an alternative behaviour, in this case the dog being calm and quiet. The exercises should be done systematically over a period of time. Positive results come quicker than you may think.

If you take classes to teach your dog this behaviour it becomes scheduled learning, the same as when you teach the dog how to sit, lie down and come when called. Problem behaviour has to be treated the same way. Create a "lesson plan", focusing on a positive way to encourage the dog to stop barking in the car.

This does not mean that you should put the dog in the car and drive around until you spot a dog on the street somewhere. You cannot train the dog and drive at the same time. You have to arrange the situation and stock up with extra if you want to successfully train your dog.

Ask one person to stand in a secluded area with their dog. Drive there and park at a distance to make sure that your dog does not see the other dog and start to bark. The other dog should not approach until you give a sign. Keep an eye on your dog and give a sign for the person to come a few steps closer.

As soon as your dog notices the other dog and begins to tense, praise it in a calming voice and give it a treat, then another and another. When your dog relaxes, give a sign to the person with the other dog to come a little closer. This person should also give his or her dog a treat, so that your dog sees it. This may also have a positive effect on your dog.

Now you should praise and give your dog some treats a few times before the other dog owner gradually comes closer.

If your dog starts barking, you have proceeded too quickly and have to start from the beginning at a greater distance. You can usually handle this in a few training sessions. After that, you will need a few extra "helpers" before the dog begins to understand the concept. It may take longer in some cases, but do not despair. Just try again at a greater distance.

This is how you gradually train your dog to allow other dogs to get closer and closer, but not too close. If, after a while, another dog can pass your car a couple of metres away without your dog barking, this is a good enough result. To have the

Barking in the car for no apparent reason

Some dogs seem to bark and whine out of sheer excitement when they go for a ride. If that is the case, stimulate the dog mentally and go for a walk prior to your journey. Also, give the dog a bone or something else to occupy itself with in the car.

other dog come right next to the car is too provocative and this requires separate training.

Should you not get the desired result, it may be wise to contact a dog psychologist who in turn could look for any underlying causes. Who knows, maybe your dog's irritation is amplified by pain, vision problems, a hormonal imbalance or something else?

BARKING AT THE DOOR

Most dogs bark when someone rings or knocks on the door. This is just a dog's way of sharing some basic information with the rest of the family. But sometimes, it might be a little too much...

When a dog barks excessively at the door, the dog owner's usual reaction is to try to silence and overpower it. But then the dog just barks even more.

The reason why a dog barks when a stranger announces his or her arrival with a knock at the door, or a ring on the doorbell, is to tell everyone in the family: "Hey, there's someone at the door! Open it!" The barking is an alarm to alert the others to join in and guard the house. And so we do. In our effort to silence the dog, we raise our voice and shout in anger.

In the dog's eyes, we are acting as expected. We come running to join it with the barking and protection of the home. In other words, we reinforce the behaviour that we want to put a stop to!

A dog will bark much less if it likes it when people visit. You can easily train the dog to feel that way. If you can make the doorbell symbolize something positive, the dog will bark less and restrict its protective behaviour.

You can easily come to terms with this problem by making sure that everyone, including family members, knocks on the door or rings the doorbell before they enter. Once inside, everyone should have a treat to give the dog. Guests should be informed beforehand that when they enter, they should look to the side, avoid eye contact with the dog, and give a treat to the dog. You can put a small cardboard box with treats next to the front door for any visitor to use. You might even invite more guests than usual just to practise this situation.

If the dog gets very excited by visitors and overdoes its greeting, it is a good idea to give your guest an empty toilet paper roll with hidden treats, to give to the dog. Then it will be occupied with that, which can help channel some of its energy.

A healthy dog may be sick

One of the most common causes of serious problem behaviour in dogs is disease and pain. The connection between an aggressive dog and pain is not always easy to accept. The dog seems healthy, but has a problem behaviour.

Unfortunately, the most common advice a dog owner might get is to try to be more in control of the problem dog, usually with hard methods: "You need to show him who's boss!"

The above advice was given to the owner of a two-year-old problematic German Shepherd before he went to see a veterinarian who really took the time to find out whether something was wrong. The vet found that the dog had a piece of hair irritating its eardrum. Another case was an aggressive female Jack Russell who had a serious injury in one of her knees, but it took over two years and visits to several vets before this was discovered.

It is not always easy to diagnose disease in a dog, because it cannot tell you how it feels. In contrast to humans, dogs have no facial expressions to show pain. They do not complain about chronic pain, but they do if they are seriously injured, for instance in an accident. A broken leg is of course relatively easy to spot when the dog starts to limp.

If dogs are sick they might withdraw and seem to want to be left alone. They may also be grumpy, and growl in situations where they did not previously. Perhaps they are unwilling to jump up on the sofa or get in the car. However, if you look closely, you can see the pain in the dog's eyes.

We are easily fooled by the fact that a dog looks healthy. Therefore, you should always keep a close eye on your dog and never disregard the possibility that it might be unwell – especially if its temperament seems to change, for example if it shows aggression or signs of withdrawal at home.

If you plan to seek help from a vet because of your dog's problem behaviour, you should make a list of all its possible

Some revealing statistics

Statistics reveal that an otherwise healthy five-year-old dog may suffer from:

- *pain from osteoarthritis: 50 percent chance, according to Patientföreningen Hundartros (29) (the Swedish association for canine osteoarthritis)*
- *back problems: 60 percent chance (11)*
- *dental problems in some form: 70 percent chance (4)*
- *disease associated with the breed: 0 to 50 percent chance (variation between breeds)*
- *old or new muscle injury: 75 percent chance (for comparison with a study on human athletes, see next section)*
- *eye problems and vision problems: unknown percentage chance. According to the American veterinarian Dr Michael Brinkman, this might be common (6)*
- *other diseases and injuries: unknown percentage chance, but probably high*

symptoms or signs of disease. This list may help the vet to start looking in the right places. The symptoms could be itching, scratching, changes in appetite, dry or loose stools, urinating more often than usual, limping, hesitation to jump up or any other unusual signs.

This is exactly what a well-trained dog psychologist does. Together with the dog owner, he or she would carefully make a "pain analysis". This involves identifying certain behaviours that can reveal that a dog is in pain. For instance, if your dog's problem behaviour varies from day to day it may be a sign of muscle or joint pain.

No person, can with certainty say that a dog is healthy! If you hear that, it is probably wrong. You can only say that no disease was found – and this in turn depends on how closely you have looked.

MUSCLE PROBLEMS

Dogs and humans are alike when it comes to muscle structure and function. Most people know how much it can hurt if you strain or pull a muscle, which results in inflammation, and how stiff you can feel after exercise or rest. This can also be applied to dogs.

Muscle weakness can occur after digging. (Photo: Shutterstock)

Dog owners who train their dogs for agility competitions usually take good care of their dogs' muscles. (Photo: Shutterstock)

In my work with problem dogs over the years, I have seen many cases where pain was the main cause of their problem behaviour. The most common pain in dogs relates to the musculoskeletal system, especially problems with the muscles, joints and back.

A muscle problem may occur for several reasons. It could be caused by muscle inflammation, straining a tendon or muscle by taking a high jump, muscel strain after having played wildly with another dog,

soreness after a strenuous walk in difficult terrain or muscle weakness after digging holes in the garden. The problems can be related to a single muscle or a muscle group. However, the legs and neck are most commonly affected.

A recent report, presented on a news programme on Swedish TV, said that 95 percent of all human athletes suffered from muscle injuries at some time during their career. A human athlete's career averages from five to fifteen years. Muscle and joint problems are the leading cause of people needing to take sick leave, closely followed by psychological problems such as stress.

Dogs, particularly young ones, are real "athletes". They run and race at full speed, stop abruptly and jump up high in the air. The risk of getting hurt is great – and especially if you consider that most dogs will not even warm up before they explode into action. Hunting dogs, for instance, can be taken directly from the car and then immediately perform at top speed in rough terrain.

It is easy for dogs to overstrain themselves when something extra fun happens. They forget about everything else and give 100 percent to the moment. When they are in the middle of having fun, they are so focused that they do not feel pain, unless it is acutely intense. It is only afterwards, when they have calmed down, that they feel the pain. A greyhound strained a foot during a race, but although the injury was quite severe, the dog did not start limping until five minutes after the race. Then he could not walk at all.

Many dogs learn to use stress as a means to help alleviate the pain. Stress causes temporary pain relief. Some dogs become over-active just to get rid of the pain, but this will also prevent a muscle injury from healing. If a dog uses stress to reduce pain, the muscle will be strained repeatedly.

The same thing happens when you let your dog play with another dog, or otherwise let it strain itself before an injury has

Warm-up and stretching are important!

Dogs that play fast and rough use as much physical energy as a soccer player. The difference is that soccer players warm up for hours before a match, and they stretch afterwards. Dogs should also do this before and after any hard physical exercise. Dog owners who train and compete in agility are good role models, because they usually take good care of their dogs' muscles.

healed properly. The dog does not feel any pain while playing. Therefore, it is very common for dogs to have long-lasting muscle problems.

I remember a case involving a German Shepherd. We determined that he had had a muscle injury for more than seven years. He was injured during a wild game when he was around seven or eight months old. When the dog was eight years old, his owners contacted me because of his severe behavioural problems.

It may take anywhere between two and six weeks of convalescence for a muscle to heal completely, depending on the seriousness of the injury. After a period of rest, you should follow up with numerous short, calm walks, preferably with a harness and a leash. I recommend supervision by a vet or physiotherapist.

BAD BACKS

Even as early as the 1970s, I noticed unexplained limping and other problems with mobility in dogs. When I started working with a dog-interested naprapath (someone who uses a therapy involving manipulation of muscles, joints and ligaments), a common denominator soon appeared, and it was the back, that is, the spine and surrounding nerves and muscles.

I learned to look at the dynamics of dogs' movements and the likelihood that this could reveal back problems. In such cases, I also consulted a naprapath. A whole new world opened up for me, where many dogs with difficult problems were cured almost completely after receiving back treatment.

During the following decade, interest in the examination and treatment of back problems in dogs spread in Sweden. Chiropractors, osteopaths, massage therapists and other physiotherapists started to specialize in dogs.

It should be emphasized that we are not talking about any disease of the spine, but instead "locking up" and displacement of vertebrae, which are also common in the human spine. A veterinarian should of course be consulted for spinal disease and injury. Should a back specialist for instance discover Wobbler disease (common in Dobermanns), or spondylosis (common in several breeds) you need to contact a veterinarian.

In the 1990s, I did a study on back problems in dogs, in collaboration with physiotherapists and my dog psychology students (11). Four hundred Swedish dogs were studied in this survey. We had advertised the study on posters in dog clubs and other places, and offered a free back examination for their dog.

At that time, it was the first and only survey of its kind. Therefore, it attracted considerable interest not only in Sweden but also worldwide. The greatest interest came from the United States, after a shorter version of the study had been published in a few places over there. So far, the study has been published in English, German, Spanish, Italian, Danish and Russian.

A number of interesting things emerged from the study, but primarily it showed that it is just as common for dogs to have back problems as it is for humans! More than sixty percent of a normal dog population suffer from mild or more severe "lock-ups" or displacements.

This means that a dog has a sixty percent chance of having back problems. However, many dogs do not seem to be bothered. Some are slightly affected, while others seem to suffer quite a lot. It is the same with people. In general, back pain is a consequence of strain of the muscles that pull across the back. This can happen for instance after an old strain or injury is aggravated or after heavy work. Many of these problems can be helped with massage and other treatments.

A bad back may be the cause of aggressive behaviour. (Photo: Shutterstock)

treatment. In general, it was clear that for any result to be permanent, treatments had to be followed up with massage and gentle exercise.

Very often, problem behaviour can be explained, in full or partially, by a back injury. According to my study, there is nearly an 80 percent chance that an aggressive dog has something wrong with its back. With shy dogs, it was close to a 70 percent chance. The figures are statistically significant. These dogs are not sick in a medical sense, but they may have irritation from tensions in the back. Many suffer from pain and their behaviour improves after treatment by a physiotherapist.

A disturbing aspect of the results was that 25 percent of the dogs in the study turned out to have problems in the neck – and many of these could be blamed on the use of collars and jerking on the leash. Dogs that pulled hard on the leash sustained neck injuries. This fact led to the use of collars being called into question (36). People are instead beginning to use a harness.

It was not a surprise that the study revealed a clear connection between back problems and behavioural problems, in particular aggression. By removing locks and dislocations, physiotherapists were able to make these dogs good tempered and harmonious.

A German Shepherd that was very aggressive towards other dogs was taken to a chiropractor. The problem behaviour disappeared after only one treatment. When some of the behaviour returned after some time, the dog only needed follow up

PTSD – post-traumatic stress disorder

The elevated level of stress that occurs after one or several shocks is called post-traumatic stress disorder, PTSD. Most people do not realize that it plagues many dogs.

If a dog suffers a shock, its behaviour may change for a short time after the unpleasant experience. Sometimes this happens gradually, and then of course it is hard to connect it with the previous trauma. The dog might start flinching at sudden noises, and show fear of things or situations it was never afraid of in the past, or begin to threaten or attack dogs or strange people. A number of problems may arise, depending on the dog's nature as well as its current and past situation.

After a severe shock, or repeated minor traumas, there will be changes in the brain. The individual becomes more sensitive and emotional. It is as though cognitive functions partially stop working. The dog now sees the world as dangerous and goes into an alert mode, being ready for danger, both physically and mentally. This state of mind must change before you can train the dog successfully.

This phenomenon is so common that you can expect anywhere from 50 to 75 percent of all dogs to suffer from post-traumatic stress disorder, in a mild or severe form. One study revealed that nearly half of the dogs living in and around cities showed symptoms similar to PTSD because of fireworks (2). Unpleasant things happen to most dogs during their lives, for instance, something accidentally hitting or falling on them, unprovoked attacks from other dogs, strange people who seem threatening. It could also be a flexi-leash bouncing back at high speed, being hit by a car, or a sudden sharp pain experienced at the grooming parlour or veterinary clinic.

EARLY SHOCKS ARE WORST

The earlier in life a dog is shocked, the worse the effect. A traumatized puppy is generally affected for life. There might be anxiety problems at first. The puppy may be afraid of people or dogs, or hesitate before going outside and visiting certain places. This fear can easily turn into aggression. In fact, many aggressive dogs have had an underlying traumatic experience.

Thirty years ago, it was difficult to help these dogs. It was the same with people suffering from shock. However, as knowledge increases of what happens in PTSD, especially in the brain, scientists are closer to a solution and a cure.

THE ROLE OF NUTRITION

In the late 1970s, I discovered that traumatized dogs seemed to need more nutrients. I began to give these dogs supplementary vitamins and minerals. After a short time, many of them changed their behaviour. They became less anxious and aggressive and were easier to train. However, this was not enough. Therefore, I tried to explore an area that was relatively unknown, that is, the connection between nutrition and behaviour.

We soon discovered that B vitamins are the most important. Vitamin B6 is involved in producing serotonin, which dampens over-activity in the brain. Several other B vitamins also have a balancing and calming effect on the organism.

Shocks seem to have a negative effect on the brain's serotonin balance. This in turn causes the emotional part of the brain to be "speeding". No one who is in such a state can act calmly and objectively, without becoming too stressed, anxious or aggressive. It is easy to understand that such a dog is not receptive to any form of training until it has regained some inner balance (14).

Help – there is a fly!

Outdoor games in the winter mean rain or snow and frozen paws. But summertime is wonderful. However, this lovely time of the year also brings challenges that may hurt or scare a dog, such as snakes, ticks, or broken glass on the ground. Buzzing insects can be added to the list of frightening things. If a wasp or a bee has stung your dog, it may never forget it.

DEVELOPMENT OF PHOBIAS

A phobia might develop purely by accident. Puppies, for instance, can get stung when they chase insects like wasps or bees. This sudden pain might be strong enough to cause a phobia.

Another reason could be that a dog owner fails to see potential dangers. While waiting to begin a search, a German Shepherd had been tied to a tree. Unfortunately, the dog owner did not notice a ground hornet's nest under the roots of the tree. A swarm of aggressive wasps attacked the

dog. After this traumatic experience, even a fly could be enough to cause the dog to panic and freak out.

I have observed this at close hand. One day, I saw a neighbour's dog tied to a long rope by a tree in the garden. Suddenly, the dog screamed and ran as far as the rope would allow it, then he came to an abrupt halt. He began to run back and forth; he was obviously totally in panic. I could not see any hornets or other dangers, but something had certainly spooked the dog. However, I knew that this dog previously

Be careful! If a puppy gets stung by a bee, the sudden pain may be strong enough to cause a phobia. (Photo: Shutterstock)

had been stung by a swarm of wasps and was traumatized by the experience. Now the buzzing of a few flies was enough to cause the dog to panic.

LOOK OUT!

It is important to keep a close watch over your dog. Is there a swarm of bees or nest of wasps nearby? Have you noticed an unusual amount of buzzing from insects in this area? Is there an anthill nearby? If you plan to sit down or tie your dog up for a few minutes, you need to scan the surroundings for anything that might scare or hurt your dog.

Do not leave the dog unattended, especially when it is tied up to something. If you cannot keep an eye on it, ask someone else to. If insects cause the dog to run in panic, it may injure itself when coming to an abrupt stop at the end of the leash. If the dog wears a collar, this could result in head and neck injuries, especially if it is wearing a choke collar. Even with a harness, there might be injuries.

A dog in this panicked state may also run around the tree to which it is tied, and the leash can then get shorter and shorter. Finally stuck, it will then try to back out of the collar, thus hurting itself even more or even strangling itself.

DIFFICULT TO CURE

I have had a number of dogs with insect phobia and they have all been very difficult to help.

Characteristic of any phobia is that a successful escape from that threat will reinforce the phobia. This is why dogs can be set off at the sight or sound of a fly. As a dog owner, you have no chance of reacting before the dog panics – and then it is too late to do anything.

If a dog has been previously traumatized by insects, you should begin "aftershock treatment" using B vitamins and herbs (14). A training programme should be carried out that includes you "mimicking" the sound of insects. You can accomplish this by recording the sound of an insect, or find a recording. Use this sound in practice sessions with the dog during the summer until it stops reacting to the sound.

Start training slowly and play the sound at such a low level that it is hardly detectable by the human ear. Gradually increase the volume, but not too fast. While the sound is playing, the dog should be busy doing something fun, for instance chewing on a bone or searching for treats. If you advance too fast, the plan may backfire. It is better to take it nice and slowly.

The phobia may return after a period. In learning psychology, this is referred to as "spontaneous recovery of the conditioned reflex". Things you had forgotten come back after a period of time. This means that you need to practise with the dog in the early spring, before the insects start to appear. Often it does not take that much time in the second year.

Some dogs are more sexual than others and will try to ride on anyone that accepts it. (Photo: Shutterstock)

Castration is not a good solution

Nowadays, it is very common to have male dogs castrated. Sometimes it is the veterinarian's first suggestion if you have a problem dog that is attacking other dogs. Other people may also suggest it.

However, the chances that this will help the problem are not very high. Statistics show that castration used as a means of stopping aggression in dogs only helps in 60 percent of cases, and a little higher when it comes to sexual fixation and exaggerated sniffing (17). You might say that it is like "shooting flies with a cannon", which means using too much power and still missing the target.

THERE ARE ADVANTAGES – BUT ALSO DISADVANTAGES

It is not easy for a mature male dog when female dogs are in heat – and this happens at least twice a year to each female. Apart from the suffering, it may

135

increase aggression towards other male dogs, lessen the appetite to the point where it is unhealthy, increase stress and make the dog start mounting people, other dogs or animals and furniture. After castration, a male dog may walk a little more easily through life.

The change in a male dog after castration can be major, and it may have unfortunate effects. The dog's appetite may grow out of control, and it may be obsessed with food as if it is constantly hungry. The dog might as well become much calmer, even lethargic. The risk of thyroid problems increases with age. Intact males may regard the neutered dog as a female and try to mate with him. For the same reason female dogs may show aggression. A few castrated male dogs also show signs of depression.

BREEDING AIMS ARE THE PROBLEM

The reason why so many dog owners choose castration is that their male dogs have become "over–masculine". For the past 25-plus years, judges in dog shows have been rewarding masculine dogs for "good sexual appearance". Dogs with a masculine look consequently get higher scores.

Given that most breeders want their dogs to score highly in competitions, they continue to breed dogs that receive the best scores from the judges. Unfortunately, it will then be the judges' view of what is beautiful that controls their breeding programmes.

A dog's appearance is the last thing you should take into consideration in breeding. On the contrary, breed-related diseases, temperament and a healthy anatomy should be more important.

In order to reach a sound basis for breeding, you should not look only at the prospective parents. The siblings of the parents, as well as close relatives, must also be included in the assessment to get an idea of what the puppies will be like. Therefore, you should not get a puppy only because the parents

Breeders should aim for physically and mentally healthy dogs instead of dogs that receive the best results at shows. (Photo: Shutterstock)

have been successful in dog shows. Instead, try to buy a puppy from a breeder who can prove that they place their emphasis on physically and mentally healthy dogs.

ETHICAL CONSIDERATIONS AND ALTERNATIVES

Castration is a procedure which may have negative consequences. To neuter a dog out of convenience because it sniffs and pees too often, or is a handful to control on walks, is unethical. Before a final decision is made, the veterinarian should talk to the dog owner about both the advantages and disadvantages of the surgery.

There is an alternative to castration and I find it strange that more vets do not suggest it. Their first choice should be chemical castration, which is a non-permanent solution. The dog gets a single injection (or a course of pills) which contains the female pregnancy hormone progesterone. This hormone has an inhibitory effect on the male sex hormone, testosterone. I usually recommend pills, because if the dog has a negative reaction, the treatment can be interrupted. The effect of a shot lasts around three months.

With this chemical alternative, you will get an idea of the dog's reaction and possible change in behaviour after real castration. Long-term use of chemical castration drugs, however, is not advisable because there may be a risk that the dog develops tumours.

Deslorelin is another hormone used in chemical castration. It stops the production of the sex hormones testosterone and oestrogen. A chip containing the hormone is inserted under the dog's skin and the effect lasts up to six months.

A number of herbs and plants contain microscopic amounts of the female hormone oestrogen. These so-called phytoestrogens will also suppress the effect of testosterone. They are for instance found in soy, St John's wort, certain lentils and sprouts, liquorice root and hops. St John's wort may also suppress anxiety and aggression. However, it should be administered under the supervision of a veterinarian, since it may affect other medication. Also, do not give St John's wort to hairless dogs, because it increases the skin's sensitivity to sunlight. Furthermore, please note that liquorice root as well as St. John's wort may increase blood pressure, so do not give these to your dog without consulting a vet.

Perhaps phytoestrogens will be the alternative first choice in future to lessen the effects of testosterone in male dogs.

This is not the final solution. We should not accept that dogs need special medication or surgery in order to function. The responsibility lies with breeders, who should produce healthy and well-functioning dogs.

(Photo: Shutterstock)

1. Anderson, S. Es.:
Pet animals and society.
British Small Animal Veterinary Assocation,
The Macmillan Publishers Company Inc.,
New York, 1975

2. Axelsson, A.:
Fyrverkerirädsla hos hund
(Fireworks phobia in dogs).
Thesis in psychology, Karlstad University, 1994

3. Benjaminsson, T.:
**Helstryp kontra sele - en studie om dess
påverkan på hunden** (Choke collar versus
harness, a study on the effects on the dog).
Thesis 331, Swedish Agricultural University,
Skara, 2010

4. Berge, E. (Norwegian veterinarian
specializing in dentistry): pers. comm. 2012

5. Blackwell, E. J., et al.:
**The relationship between training methods
and the occurrence of behavior problems,
as reported by owners, in a population of
domestic dogs.**
Journal of Veterinary Behavior: Clinical
Applications and Research, Volume 3, issue 5,
207–217, 2008

6. Brinkman, M.:
Optik no. 1/2005
(Swedish trade magazine for opticians)

7. Diamond, M.:
**Extensive cortical depth measurements and
neuron size increases in the cortex of
environmentally enriched rats.**
Journal of Comparative Neurology,
Volume 131, Issue 3, 357–364, 1967

8. Dickey R. A., Parker J. L. & Feld S.:
**Discovery of unsuspected thyroid
pathologic conditions after trauma to the
anterior neck area attributable to a motor
vehicle accident: relationship to use of the
shoulder harness. Endocrine Practice,**
Jan–Feb; Volume 9, Issue 1, 5–11, 2003

9. Ekman, H.:
Vargen (The Wolf).
Nordstedts förlag, Stockholm 2010

10. Friedmann, E., et al.:
**Effect of a pet on cardiovascular responses
during communication by coronary prone
individuals.**
In: Living Together: People, Animals and the
Environment; Delta Society Conference, 1986

11. Hallgren, A.:
**Rückenprobleme beim Hund,
Untersuchungsreport. (Back problems in
dogs, research report)**
Animal Learn Verlag, Bernau, 2003

12. Hallgren, A.:
**Gute Arbeit – über die Eignung und
Motivation von Arbeitshunden. (Good work!
- Drive and motivation of working dogs)**
Animal Learn Verlag. Bernau, 2005

13. Hallgren, A.:
Das Alpha-Syndrom. (The alpha syndrome)
Animal Learn Verlag. Bernau, 2006

14. Hallgren, A.:
Stress, Anxiety and Aggression in Dogs
Cadmos Publishing, Richmond, 2012

15. Hallgren, A.:
Mental Activation
Cadmos Publishing, Richmond, 2008

16. Harlow, H. F.:
Love in infant monkeys.
Scientific American, Volume 200, 68–74, 1959

17. Hart, B. L. & Hart, L. A.:
Canine and Feline Behavior Therapy.
Lea & Febiger, Philadelphia, 1985

18. Hiby, E. F. et al.:
**Dog training methods: their use, effective-
ness and interaction with behaviour and
welfare.**
Animal Welfare, Volume 13, 63–69, 2004

19. Iacoboni, M.:
The New Science of Empathy and How We Connect with Others.
Picador, Farrar, Straus and Giroux, New York, 2008

20. Jensen, P.: personal communication, 2012

21. Langer, E. & Rodin, J.:
The effects of choice and enhanced personal responsibility for the aged: A field experiment in an institutional setting.
Journal of Personality and Social Psychology, Volume 34, Issue 2, 191–198, 1976

22. Levinson, B.:
Pet-Oriented Child Psychotherapy.
Charles C. Thomas, Publisher, Illinois, 1969

23. Lockard, J. S.:
Choice of a warning signal or no warning signal in an avoidable shock situation.
Journal of Comparative and Physiological Psychology Volume 56, 526–530, 1969. Cited in Jensen, P. (ed.): The Behavioural Biology of Dogs, CAB International, Oxfordshire, 2007

24. Magnusson, E.:
Parental investment hos tamhund
(Parenthal investment by domestic dogs).
D/E-thesis, Department of Zoology, Stockholm University, 1981

25. Malm, K.:
Dominans, ett problem av rang. (Dominance, a high-ranking problem)
Hundsport, No. 11/93. The Swedish Kennel club magazine, Stockholm, 1993

26. Mech, D.:
The wolf.
Natural History Press, Garden City, N.Y., 1970

27. Miklósi, Á.:
Dog Behaviour, Evolution and Cognition.
Oxford University Press, USA, 2008

28. Murie, A.:
The wolves of Mount McKinley.
U.S. Dept. Intl. Fauna Series, No. 5, Washington, US Government Printing Office, 1944

29. Patientföreningen Hundartros
(Swedish association for dog osteoarthritis):
www.hundartros.se

30. Pauli, A. M., Bentley, E., Diehl, K. A., Miller, P. E.:
Effects of the application of neck pressure by a collar or a harness on intraocular pressure in dogs.
Journal of the American Animal Hospital Association, Volume 42, Issue 3, 207–211, 2006

31. Rowell, T. E.:
The concept of social dominance.
Behavior Biology, Volume II, 131–154, 1974

32. Schilder, M. & van der Borg, J.:
Training dogs with help of the shock collar; short and long term behavioural effects.
Applied Animal Behavior Science, Volume 85, 319–334, 2004

33. Seligman, M.:
Helplessness: On Depression, Development and Death.
Freeman, San Francisco, 1975

34. Thoresen, A.: Personal communication, 2009

35. Zimen, E.:
The Wolf – a Species in Danger.
Delacorte Press, New York, 1981

36. www.sagnej.n.nu

37. www.assistenthunden.se

38. Weiss, J. M.:
Psychological factors in stress and disease.
Scientific American, Volume 22, 104–113, 1972

39. White, K.:
The Pixie Club for slow learners.
Society for Animal Companion Studies (SCAS) Newsletter. No. 5, 1983

40. Wilson, E.:
Maternal effects in behavior of juvenile and adult dogs.
PhD Thesis, Department of Zoology, Stockholm University, 1997

(Photo: Maurer)

INDEX